A History of Redhill

Volume One
The town from its earliest beginnings
to the end of the 19th century

Alan Moore

First published October 1999
© Alan Moore

Page design by Alan Moore
Cover design by Purple
Reprographics by Digital Impact
Printed by Grapevine Print, Worthing, West Sussex

Published by Alan Moore

A History of Redhill - Volume One
Contents

Preface

This book is about the history of Redhill from the days long before it was even the remotest twinkle in its founding fathers' eyes to the end of the nineteenth century, close to the end of Queen Victoria's reign. By this time Redhill had become a thriving town that rivalled and had even outgrown its much older close neighbour of Reigate.

A facet of local history is that the whole story is contained in various sources that are not always easy to seek out. Much information is in a multiplicity of old documents and other material stored at sites, some public, some private, usually miles apart. Much more is in the memories of people whose reminiscences of times past are too valuable not to write down. This book assembles more information about Redhill than has ever before been gathered together in one place at one time. It sketches a picture of events long past that laid the basis for much of what we see around us today.

Individual chapters deal with early roads, industry, buildings, institutions, churches and other aspects of the town, including its growth from almost a swamp to a small habitation known as Warwick Town. How the development of the railway and other influences created Redhill is explained, and the book takes a long look at the formation of the town and the struggle to pull it and its sister town of Reigate out of the grip of the Lords of the Manor and place control of people's lives in the hands of an accountable alternative that is the modern system of local government we have today.

Included are many of the issues that the town has seen as crucial to its development, from the granting of a Charter of Incorporation to the creation of Borough Police and Fire Services, with personal reminiscences of people who knew the town in its earliest days.

The book begins with a foreword by fellow local historian, Roger Ellaby, that details the events from pre-history to the emergence of Reigate as a market town and chief influence in the district in the twelfth century. The story of Redhill starts with its appearance as a newcomer and rival to Reigate seven hundred years later. It continues through fifteen chapters and more than one hundred and twenty-five pictures and illustrations. While many subjects are complete through to the present day, this volume generally tells the story up to the end of the 19th century. Work on a companion volume continuing this history of Redhill into living memory and to the Millennium and beyond has already begun.

<u>Front Cover:</u>

The present St John's School, Pendleton Road, has its origins in a school built opposite the church in 1845. Comparison with the rear view picture of the original building on page 44 shows fairly good agreement of detail, except perhaps for the position of the two side chimneys. A clock tower was added, probably around 1860, the date of the still existing clock. Nothing of the pictured building remains, the part of the school now seen from Pendleton Road dating from 1884 and the existing upper building from 1910. (Picture courtesy St John's School)

Acknowledgements

In the course of the years during which my growing interest in the history of Redhill became a full-blooded quest for written, pictorial and material remnants of the past, I have met a great many people who have contributed enthusiasm, information, reminiscences and encouragement. To name them all is an impossible task, for not only would I unintentionally but inevitably omit someone but also there is simply not enough room for all their names in these pages.

I hope, however, that the unnamed majority does not mind if I pick out just a few people for individual mention. Thanks go to Roger Packham, Chairman of the Bourne Society, for his encouragement and assistance; Sean Hawkins for advice and yet more encouragement; and Steve Kulka, who advised and assisted greatly with the necessary technology with which I created this book, whilst remaining patiently tolerant of my basic ignorance of it.

I must not omit special mention of all the previous historians and other observers of the local scene who have provided valuable works of reference. I also extend thanks to certain organisations that hold valuable historical information, and I gratefully acknowledge the material they so kindly gave me access to. A list of these appears on page 157.

Roger Ellaby kindly agreed to assist with proof reading and presentation aspects of the book in its final stages. He also generously supplied additional informative and authoritative text in the form of a foreword that I am delighted to include. Special thanks to Roger.

Finally, there are some people who are sadly no longer here to be thanked, and who, when I look back, had a special impact upon me and my growing interest. These include Ben Keenan, who was always full of cheerful, enthusiastic, knowledgeable and spontaneous interest, and was a Redhill man through and through; Charlie Reason, a Reigate man to his boots; Jack Sales, who saw so much through the eye of his camera; and Wally Shipton, of whom, as with the others, I asked far too few questions when I had the chance to do so.

Without the help I have received from all of the above this book would not have been possible, and because this acknowledgement seems so inadequate I sincerely hope the story within its pages says it better.

Thank you all.

Alan Moore, October 1999

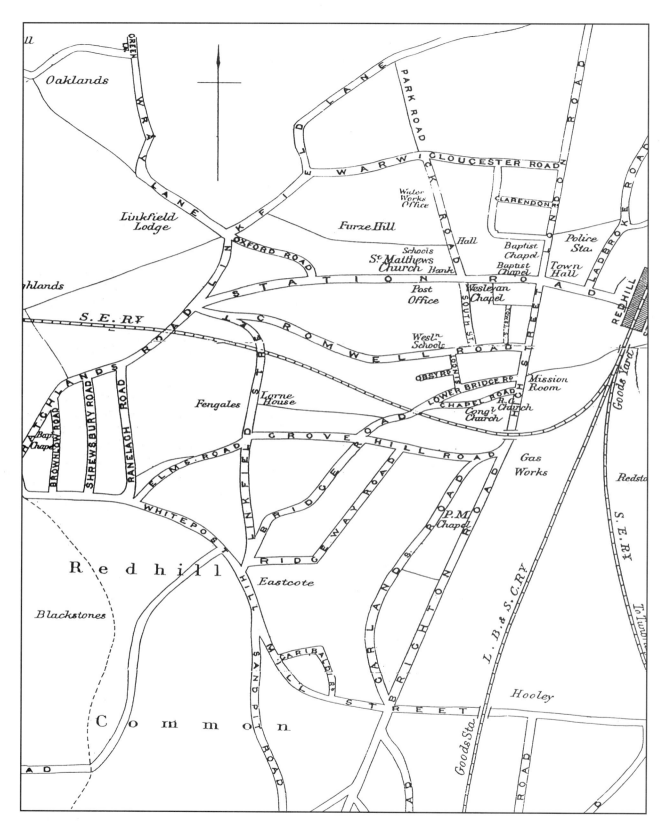

A developing Redhill during the reign of Queen Victoria, with the road pattern and names mostly as we know them today (After Phillips, 1885)

The Beginning Of It All

A Foreword by Roger Ellaby

The history of Redhill is but a moment compared to the aeons that passed over this small part of the world before the town appeared. To many it may seem superfluous to mention this past but it must be remembered that our environment and way of life are a result of all that has gone before. This foreword, necessarily brief, abridged and conjectural, deals with those principal events preceding the times that the main body of this book will dwell upon at length.

Geology and landscape

Redhill is situated on the northern edge of the Weald on Lower Greensand, a marine deposit laid down in the time of the dinosaurs one hundred million years ago. These sands were preceded by a freshwater sediment of Weald Clay and succeeded by further marine deposits of Gault Clay, Upper Greensand and Chalk. These layers of sediment were then uplifted into the great Wealden dome by the same earth movements that created the Alps. Over millions of years the dome was eroded by streams, rivers and hillwash, re-exposing the old layers of sediment and carving the landscape of hills and valleys we know today.

Early people

In the latest stages of this erosion the earliest people arrived on the scene. Over perhaps half a million years small bands of hunter-gatherers occasionally visited the Redhill/Reigate area, leaving as flimsy evidence of their passing a flint handaxe found on Redhill Common and another from Woodhatch. Much material from this period, however, has probably been washed away by erosional forces.

It is only since the end of the last Ice Age, when the landscape reached its present form, that considerable evidence of early visitors has survived. Indeed, during the earliest phase of the development of Redhill town, in 1857, a local antiquary, John Shelley, picked up many thousands of flint artefacts from a spot now below the car park of Redhill railway station. The flints were discarded by a band of Mesolithic hunter-gatherers who had camped beside a lake ten thousand years ago. Flints of this period have been recovered from several places in the district, as also have those from the Neolithic period when the first farmers arrived about six thousand years ago. Permanent settlement probably began in the succeeding Bronze Age, and artefacts from this period and the following Iron Age and Romano-British phases have also been discovered.

The Saxons

The next settlers, from the fifth or sixth century AD, were the Saxons who probably arrived in the district from the Thames valley. From a vantage point on Reigate Hill we can imagine them looking down into the vale below and seeing a land laid bare of any extensive woodland by many years of use by farmers and industrialists. This landscape stood in contrast to the sweep of Wealden forest to the south and they called it *Cherchefelle*, 'The open land below the hill.'

The Saxons were to carve out of this land an estate of the same name, which in time merged with adjacent estates to form the great Manor of Cherchefelle. It reached to the boundaries of Gatton and Kingswood in the north, Betchworth and Buckland in the west, Nutfield in the east and the Wealden forest to the south into which fingers of land extended for the benefits of timber and the fattening of pigs on acorns and beechmast. The original estates, headed by Cherchefelle, were Linkfield (in which the modern town of Redhill was to be situated), Colley, Santon, Woodhatch and Hooley. They became the boroughs or tithings of the Manor, the administrative districts that endured for perhaps a thousand years until their demise in the nineteenth century.

1066

On the eve of the Norman Conquest, in 1066, Cherchefelle was a relatively wealthy Manor dotted with farmsteads, probably with a church on the site of the present St Mary Magdalene's and the beginning of a small 'town' close by. The Manor was in royal hands, recently bequeathed to Queen Edith, wife of the Saxon king Edward the Confessor who died in that year. Queen Edith held the Manor for nine years after the Conquest until her death in 1075 when the property returned to the Crown. In c1088 it was granted to William de Warenne, one of the principal knights of William the Conqueror at the Battle of Hastings. A successor, probably William de Warenne II, built a castle on the Manor partly as a symbol of power over

the local Saxon population and partly as a residence for the Lord when visiting Cherchefelle for progress reports. (The de Warennes were absentee landlords and held land in many parts of England. Their chief seat was Lewes Castle in Sussex).

The rise of Reigate

The de Warennes were powerful Lords and there was no way they were going to allow Cherchefelle to fall into decay. Around 1150 the old Saxon 'town' near the church was abandoned and a new town planned and constructed below the castle. Like many towns and villages that arose in England at this time it was designed to act as a focal point for trade and commerce and thus to increase the wealth of the Manor and, of course, its Lord. The new town, which also gave its name to the old Manor of Cherchefelle, was called Reigate, 'roe-deer gate', possibly an allusion to its siting at the entrance to, or on the boundary of, the de Warenne's deer park (now Reigate Park and Priory Park).

A new kid on the block

Reigate remained the only town in the district for the next seven hundred years, its influence affecting the lives of all who lived within the Manor bounds. On the eastern side of the Manor, in the tithing of Linkfield, the inhabitants lived in farmsteads and hamlets dispersed around a low-lying area traversed by streams. It was in this depression, at the end of the Ice Age, that hunter-gatherers had camped beside a lake in a land of birchwood, elk and beaver. Over the centuries, however, the lake became choked with vegetation and peat until by the middle of the nineteenth century AD it remained as a quaking bog. Out of this bog grew the hub of a surprising new town with a surprising name - Redhill.

Why and how did this new town, and its name, emerge? How did it evolve? How did its inhabitants live? How did Reigate react to its new upstart neighbour? These questions and many more will be answered in the following pages of Alan Moore's illuminating history of Redhill.

Reigate from the south many years before Redhill began its existence as a companion town close to the North Downs of Surrey. (Palgrave, 1860)

MUTTON'S

Commercial and Family . . **HOTEL,**

HIGH STREET, REDHILL.

HOT LUNCHEONS DAILY. BATHS ALWAYS READY.

Splendid Accommodation for Cyclists. The best known House on the Brighton Road. Recommended by Cyclists' Touring Club.

Proprietor: ALF. C. MUTTON, Consul C.T.C.

The Early Roads

A picture taken in 1800 of the area south of Gatton where modern Redhill now is, would show a great deal of clumpy growth on low lying marshland which attracted wildlife but not man. Roads avoided the area but even the many miles of roads that existed elsewhere in the Manor were less than desirable thoroughfares for wheeled vehicles, making travel a problem.

The ancient routes that had crossed the Manor for hundreds of years were well defined. The east-west route followed the high ground from Bletchingley and Nutfield, descended Redstone Hollow, followed Hooley Lane, passed over Red Hill Common via Mill Street and Whitepost Hill to Shaws Corner, before continuing towards Reigate along Reigate Road.

At the junction of Mill Street and Whitepost Hill a northerly route led down Linkfield Street and into Linkfield Lane before continuing into Wiggey Street, now Frenches Road, and on to Merstham via Battlebridge Lane. If the traveller did not want to go to Nutfield via Nutfield Marsh, nor take the spur towards Chilmead Farm - the Cormongers Lane of today - he would turn towards what is now School Hill. This was once an extension of Merstham High Street at a time when the existing road, the present A23 London - Brighton Road, did not exist. Instead the road ran onwards along Quality Street and up Merstham Hill towards London.

A southerly route from the junction of Mill Street and Whitepost Hill probably passed across the common via Sandpit Lane and Common Road, past the present Albatross public house and the old golf clubhouse. A northerly route from the same point followed part of Linkfield Lane to Batts Hill, crossed Wray Common and ascended Wray Lane.

The other south-north route lay through Reigate, following the current route of the A217 from Sidlow, through Woodhatch and into the town. The tunnel was not made until 1823, so the High Street and today's London Road carried traffic to the foot of Reigate Hill. The hill was the town's big problem and a number of ways up and over it existed before the making of the present road under the Suspension Bridge. Other very old roads in the area linked small communities to church and farm but were often accessible by foot only.

It had long been recognised that the local movement of herds of animals was not the only traffic, for trade had been growing. Produce had to be got to market and people had to be attracted to those towns in which the markets took place. If the roads were impassable for heavy wagons, or if people were dissuaded from going to town because of their poor condition, then trade suffered. We still have problems with our transport system in the 20th century; except that it is now mainly volume of traffic that is the trouble. The remedies are broadly the same, however, with heavier and heavier loads to be hauled along faster and more frequently if commerce is to flourish. Environmental issues apart, new roads cost money, and their funding is a big issue, with the subject of tolls never quite going away. In the past this is how many of our roads were paid for, they were turnpiked; that is gates were placed across certain roads and people were charged a toll for

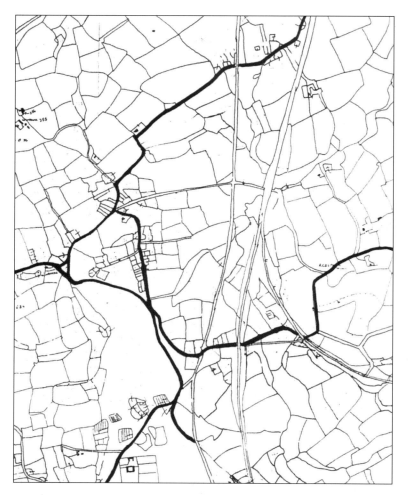

This 1844 map provides a snapshot of the almost completely rural area where Warwick Town was just about to appear as the forerunner of the modern day Redhill. The 1818 London-Brighton Road has the recently built Brighton Railway parallel with it, and the S.E.R's even newer Dover line is also shown. The new access road (the present Station Road) completes a crossroads where the centre of Redhill now is.

The main ancient roads are in bold. The road from Reigate is on the left, Union (Pendleton) Road passes the workhouse at the bottom, Linkfield Lane crosses the new road and proceeds along Wiggey Street towards Merstham at the top. Mill Street and Hooley Lane also cross the new road to go north up Redstone Hollow and then turn east towards Nutfield. Map features include field patterns and some other roads. (Based on 1844 tithe map)

their use depending on whether they were pedestrian, equestrian, drover or wagon driver.

The first turnpiked road in Surrey was the one from Reigate to Crawley. An Act of 1697 authorised the counties of Surrey and Sussex to appoint surveyors to carry out repair work, and receivers to collect tolls for its use in order to recoup the expense. The road was described as being, *'very ruinous and almost impassable for above three miles in Reigate.'* Repairs were duly put in hand and receivers of tolls stationed. Tolls were fixed, *'for all such horses, carts, coaches, waggons, droves and gangs of cattel as in time to come shall pass, be led or droven in or through the said ways.'*

In 1755 another Act authorised a body to be set up to repair the Sutton to Povey Cross road via Reigate and Sidlow. The Turnpike Trustees had their first meeting in the Swan Inn at Reigate in April, 1755, and they and their successors had regular meetings until the 1880s when the turnpike system came to an end. The first meeting dealt with the erecting of tollhouses, as well as tollgates, on the road. The gates at Woodhatch were erected in 1755, as was a tollhouse, the provision of which was directed, *'not to exceed £40 in the whole'*.

In 1796 a bill was proposed to make a new turnpike road from Purley through Merstham to Reigate, but did not become law until 1807. The road was built in 1808 by a rival trust to the Reigate one, the part from Merstham to Wray Common being made on land taken from Gatton. This road brought great change to Merstham and became part of today's London-Brighton Road. It provided an alternative connection to and from London for Reigate, and probably breathed new life into that town. The southern part of the road from Coulsdon turned west at Gatton Point, still avoiding that low-lying marshland south of Merstham and east of Reigate.

At the same time as the Reigate to Merstham and Purley road had been proposed, so had a branch from Gatton to Povey Cross. This road would continue from a point south of Gatton - possibly the origin of the name 'Gatton Point' - southwards through the marsh. It is said that the reason for building this road was to provide the Prince Regent with a route that brought his Brighton residence within the 50 mile limit stipulated by a hostile Act of Parliament. It was on this latest of the turnpike roads that there were two sets of gates locally, one at Frenches, where the new road crossed the old road from Merstham by way of Battlebridge Lane and Linkfield Lane to join the old Godstone-Reigate road near what is now Reffells Bridge, the other at Salfords on the corner of Honeycrock Lane. The Act for constructing this road was passed in 1816, and was opposed by Earl Somers, then Lord of the Manor of Reigate, partly because he did not want a road bisecting his estates, but mainly because it would divert traffic from his town of Reigate, and thereby lose money for those who benefited from the trade generated by it, himself among them.

A surveyor to the turnpike trustees had under his management the section of the road through Reigate from Sutton on the north to the county boundary at Lowfield Heath, and to meet the competition of the alternative route certain improvements were made to this ancient way.

Above is shown the triple set of tollgates at Woodhatch, the first view looking towards Prices Lane, the second towards the Angel. Right are the gates at the Yew Tree, Reigate Hill.

A coach passing though the tollgates on Reigate Hill.

A cut was made from Sidlow to Hookwood Common, thereby avoiding the old detour and the hill at Horse Hills. Cockshot Hill was lowered and the spoil employed in raising the High Street of Reigate. The Lesbourne, which formerly crossed Bell Street in an open watercourse, was culverted, and the detour by the Red Cross was eventually avoided by the tunnel under the castle. By these means the attractiveness to traffic of the old, original road was partially preserved, but means were also employed to reduce the attractiveness to traffic on the new road.

The road as originally planned was to run through Earlswood parallel with the brook to near the present site of the Earlswood Asylum, avoiding the nearby hill. Earl Somers secured the services of the same surveyor who was working on the old road, and who, on his Lordship's behalf, contrived another route which would take a dog-leg right at the present Reading Arch to ascend the hill, now the Brighton Road, and pass close to where St. John's Church now is. The route would continue southwards across the 'switchback' on Earlswood Common. The surveyor intentionally avoided making full plans with a section so that the re-routed road's hilliness was not plain to the Parliamentary Committee examining and approving the plans.

The ploy worked, and although the cutting through Lord Somers' Hooley estate was not wholly avoided, the level route originally designed was not adhered to, and 'old crocks' on the London to Brighton run have often required a push up a hill when they might have had a far easier ride on the flat route the railway was to take a few years later. It has been reported that Lord Somers remarked to his surveyor, 'Well, Mr Constable, you have spoiled their road.'

The new road, through its saving of distance and in spite of its hill, still attracted a large portion of Reigate's post and coaching traffic. To accommodate it (and make money from it) a new inn was built on the corner of Mill Street and the Brighton Road, appropriately called 'The Somers Arms'. The original building still stands and today is called 'The Firs'. In what proportions the traffic was divided between the two towns is not clear, but one account of the traffic volume stated, '*in the eighteen thirties it was impossible to go half a mile upon either road without passing some coach or carriage*', a statement intended to convey the frequency of traffic and which now makes ironic comparison with the amount of traffic encountered today.

A Coach at the White Hart Hotel, Reigate, in the days before the road through what is now Redhill was made.

Coaches and carriages had no brakes in those days, and the skidpan, a wooden wedging device locking the wheels on the road, was used. There was a man by the name of Brown who had a shelter at the crown of the hill at Earlswood. When a coach drove up he would skid the wheel for the driver, jump up behind the coach and travel with it until the steepest part of the descent had been negotiated. Then he would dismount and, with his skid pan, walk back, or maybe get a free ride on a return coach, to his shelter to await the next job. He became a noted character, well known to coach drivers and others, and found his reward in the small coins thrown to him by travellers.

Probably this same method was used down Reigate Hill too, but getting up that particular hill was a double problem that had a double solution. The steepness was overcome by attaching an extra pair of horses, hired in the town, to give extra pulling power, the additional pair being unhitched at the top and returned to the staging point, often the White Hart Inn, ready for the next coach. The second problem was that coach wheels sank into the unmetalled road surface, especially after rain. The remedy for this was the laying in 1839 of twin 'tram tracks' made of granite on which the coach wheels could run on the steepest part of the hill. So successful was this that the following year it was ordered that a further two hundred yards of granite track be added. It was paid for by, '*individuals feeling an interest in the work*', which probably meant coach and hotel proprietors and others who made money out of the passing trade. No evidence has come to light of such remedies being employed on the hilly part of the rival road through what is now Redhill.

The London to Brighton railway, opened in the early 1840s, spelled the end for coaching traffic. It also seriously damaged the incomes of those businesses which depended upon it. The Somers Arms Inn closed and its sign, it is said, was taken down and transferred to the Somers Arms at Reffells Bridge.

Times were changing.

Road Names

Prior to the introduction of postal services few roads had names. The

Fresh horses and shovels being brought to rescue a coach off the Brighton Road at Earlswood in winter.

exceptions were those that led to other towns and places, such as Reigate Road, Dorking Road, London Road, and so on. New roads began to have names and old ones were given names for the first time to aid the delivery of letters.

Names once given were sometimes changed for a variety of reasons. Pendleton Road was once called Union Road because it led to a workhouse, or 'Union'. The change was made after the workhouse closed around 1938. The new name was presumably after Mr E.C.P.Hull (the P standing for Pendleton) who lived at the Mount, a large house across from the workhouse. In 1882

Gatton Road, Redhill, probably so named because Gatton was visible from it, was renamed Grove Hill Road.

At the same time Holmesdale Road at South Park became St Luke's Road; Holmesdale Road, Meadvale, became Lower Road; Somers Road, South Park, was changed to Eastnor Road and Warren Road, Meadvale, became Copse Road. The reason for these changes was that the old names were duplications of road names that existed elsewhere in the Borough. It was at this time that the old name of Mead Hole, long since out of popular use, was officially changed to Meadvale.

Extra horses attached to a coach on Reigate Hill. By having to pass around slower traffic the coach is not getting the benefit of the 'tramways', which can be clearly seen.

Putting the 'Mill' back into Mill Street

One of the intriguing facets of local history is that not everything can be neatly explained, and Mill Street, which today starts at the top of Whitepost Hill and ends at the Brighton Road, but once continued down what is now Hooley Lane, presents us with a small puzzle. The puzzle is that when the name 'Mill' is associated with a thoroughfare it would normally indicate that a mill of some kind, if not still there once existed very close by, and that the road or lane in question led directly to it. Mill Way, close to Shaws Corner, once led up to the Blackborough mill, and there is proof of the mill on maps of the period. Unfortunately this is not the case where Redhill's Mill Street is concerned, because not only is there not a mill in existence now but there never has been very much evidence that one was ever there.

Although documentary proof was always lacking a belief of the existence of a water mill beside the brook in Earlswood has always abounded, as has speculation that if it did indeed exist then its demise would have come about in 1840/41 when the London-Brighton railway was built across Hooley Lane. Dr Clair Grece, Redhill's first Town Clerk, contributed an article to the Surrey Mirror in 1897, the year of Queen Victoria's Diamond Jubilee, in which he wrote about the building of the railway. Hooley Lane and the brook under it underwent certain changes, he said, the lane being straightened, the stream diverted and the old packhorse bridge over the brook being replaced by a new bridge at a different point.

Dr Grece also referred to a Victorian poetess, Eliza Cook, saying that one of two poems written by her about gypsies was inspired by the tented dwellers inhabiting the horse pound at the other end of Hooley Lane, where the road divides between the present Philanthropic Road and Redstone Hollow. This would indicate that Eliza Cook knew the area well, seemingly confirmed in the 1897 article when Dr Grece refers to Eliza Cook getting this knowledge when she lived in Hooley.

The old pack horse bridge across the Redhill brook at Hooley Lane
(Courtesy Surrey Mirror)

Eliza possibly lived at a house once called 'The Water House', later known as 'Brook Glen'. Corroboration for this comes from a one time editor of the Surrey Mirror, Mr Charles W. Preston, in whose collection of notes on local people he says that she lived there in 1845; and from an old resident of Hooley Lane who, when met once by Guy Bingham, also of the Surrey Mirror, said that her father had known Eliza Cook well.

This is not direct evidence of the existence of a mill of course, but Eliza Cook did write other poems, two of them especially appropriate. In 'The Old Watermill', Eliza writes graphically of remembered school days: -

> *And is this the old millstream that ten years ago*
> *Was so fast in its current, so pure in its flow,*
> *Whose musical waters would ripple and shine,*
> *With the glory and dash of a miniature Rhine?*

And she introduces the miller........

> *Forgetting grey hairs was as loud in his mirth*
> *As the veriest youngster that circled the hearth.*

And the mill...

> *....................where we idled away*
> *Our holiday hours on a clear summers day;*
> *Where Roger, the Miller's dog, lolled on a sack*
> *And chorused his song to the merry click-clack.*

> ...of the mill machinery?

And a rather sad part......

> *But lo! what sacrilege here has been done?*
> *The streamlet no longer purls on in the sun;*
> *Its course has been turned and its desolate edge*
> *Is now mournfully covered with duckweed and sedge.*

> ....as it would be if the stream had been diverted for part of its course or reduced in volume.

Another poem, 'The Old Mill Stream', refers to Eliza's memories of the stream in her youth, of fishing for trout in it, of it being covered in ice in winter, and of the ford.......

> *Where mounted on Dobbin we youngsters would dash,*
> *Both pony and rider enjoying the splash.*

Are these poems about a mill that is supposed to have existed on the banks of the nearby Redhill Brook? It has been suggested that this is just what they are about, but if Eliza Cook had the memories portrayed in the poem she would have had to have seen the mill in its heyday and been familiar with the area from earlier than 1845, and at that latter date have been making a return visit, which is claimed to have been the case. Eliza was born in 1818, so this is quite possible, and in 1845 she would have been 26 or 27 years of age. She writes of the millstream being in decline, which it might well have been after the railway works, and by various associations more than suggests the existence of a mill during her childhood.

However enjoyable as this speculation in support of the reality of the mill is it seems that Eliza's father kept a shop in Southwark, and without evidence of relatives in Hooley where she could have spent some of her childhood and revisited later in life, the mill at this point will have to remain a possibility only.

'Brook Glen', or 'The Water House', where Eliza Cook is said to have written her poems, and which stood about where Earlsbrook Road now joins Hooley Lane.

Perhaps Eliza's desire to write poetry precluded absolute accuracy, and a stream in decline might have given rise to the notion of a mill in imagination only, poetic licence running, therefore, to fictionalisation.

At least one other author has made note of the poems of Eliza Cook in relation to defunct water mills. In 'On Surrey Hills' written in 1892 by 'A Son of the Marshes', otherwise Mr Denham Jordan, the once well known author who finished his life in 1920 in obscurity in Dorking Union Infirmary, is written:

'There are quiet and beautiful nooks beside the woodland Mole. Here and there are the ruins of some old mill which was once busy and full; and you can trace through the meadows the spot where a mill pond had its source. The meadow lies even now two, or sometimes even four feet, below the banks of what was once the pond. Even the walls of the sluice gates remain, covered with ferns and mosses of varied tints. One of these it was that suggested Eliza Cook's poem, 'The Old Water Mill', ... Although modern improvements have destroyed much of the picturesqueness of rural life, there is still plenty of it left, if one knows where to look for it. This was a favourite haunt, during her childhood, of the poetess who has so recently gone to her rest. She loved this old mill and wrote of it more than once.'

This passage is geographically and otherwise very general. On the one hand the described locations could be anywhere, on the other the reader gets the impression of a particular site. As this book and Eliza's poems are now over one hundred years behind us we cannot ask, so on these matters must continue to speculate.

Fortunately more speculation is possible, for the deeds of a house in Woodlands Road show that on 27th June, 1839, a section of land was sold to the Railway Company. This land was described as being the Hooley Park Estate, and was detailed in a number of schedules. The land in the first schedule was farmed by one Thomas Burt, and the land in the second schedule was to be used for the proposed railway. Other schedules dealt with land ownership. Details of the first schedule describes, *'a mansion called Hooley House with lawn, plantation, barns, outbuildings, yards and garden',* and goes on to list a number of fields, among which is 'Colmonger's Mill Field East' and 'West Colmonger's Mill Field'. Other fields include 'Water Meadow' and 'Mill Street Mead'.

This 1839 sale of land is exactly at the time of the supposed demise of the mill of which the speculation is all about, and the names do not seem those that would be given to fields that never saw a mill. And certainly not a windmill at such a low location, for only a watermill would fit the bill with the brook so close and a field called Water Meadow.

Completely separate from the above documents are some other, older, ones, which have been quoted as evidence that a new channel was to have been cut, 'for a new stream through the lower part of the Mill Grove and the horselease next the brook.....to carry the same into Dowsehill for the use of a watermill there to be erected.' These documents have not been seen by this author but the reference noted that Mill Grove was said to have been near to the site of the present day Redhill railway station, which would move the mill site away from Earlswood. The timing is fairly good, however, as one of the men named in the document is said to have died in 1750, so if the mill referred to was built, it could well have still been around at the same time as Eliza Cook.

In spite of the evidence discussed here we are still no nearer to the absolute proof that is required to site the mill somewhere nearby. What actually is happening is that a mill is wanted and all available evidence is being matched to it in a way that would make its existence as viable as possible, an interesting exercise, but what is really needed is a map with 'Mill' writ bold upon it.

On the other hand there are no doubt those romantics among us who might ask what more evidence is required than a road called Mill Street?

On this 1839 plan the road to Brighton runs left to right to its junction with Mill Street. Redhill Brook runs beside it before turning to cross the proposed railway, pass by buildings and then cross the road at the pack horse bridge with a ford either side. Hooley Lane is now straight from the crossroads to the second bridge just before Redstone Hollow, but the old dogleg can clearly be seen just after the rail crossing. The heavy lines enclosing part of the railway, with the bulge of a larger area to the left, enclose land bought by the rail company.

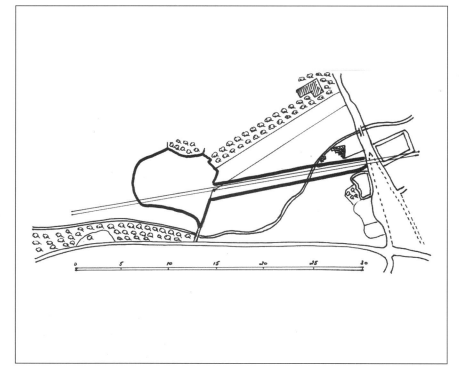

Pre-Redhill Buildings

Just because there was a time when Redhill had never been thought of does not mean that everyone lived within the bounds of Reigate Town. Although by today's standards practically everywhere outside of a town was rural there still existed within the countryside some smaller places of habitation other than individual farmsteads. Inhabited areas needed roads, so it is no surprise that along the older, more established routes, some of the area's oldest houses are to be found, houses which, in some cases, pre-date Redhill by many years.

Little London was one of these inhabited areas. This was the ironic name given to describe the litter of houses that had been put up piecemeal in an area of the common now known as St. John's. It existed before the church and school were built and was to grow considerably when the London to Brighton road and the railways were made. The development around St John's Church is today designated as a local conservation area because of the number of sites of special interest there. Among these 16 -18th century buildings, and tucked away almost out of sight, is a charming timber framed cottage that if better known might be one of Redhill's most photographed buildings. A number of houses in the nearby part of Pendleton Road date from the 16th, 17th and 18th centuries. Two of the cottages in Fountain Road are 18th century. St John's Church itself was originally built in 1843 and rebuilt in 1889-95. St John's School was first built in 1845 but also rebuilt, and it is doubtful if anything of the original remains.

Old cottages at St John's.

Fengates House for sale in 1925

In 1794 the workhouse was built not far away. It was the result of the measure known as Gilbert's Act, which enabled two or more parishes to unite in order to provide it, the parishes of Reigate Old Borough, Reigate Foreign, Horley, Nutfield and Headley coming together to form a Poor Law Union (hence Union Road). The site subsequently became the Redhill General Hospital and is today a housing estate still surrounded by the wall that used to enclose the workhouse and separate it from the surrounding common land.

Older than the workhouse and close to St John's School are Carter's Cottages, or Carter's Row (apparently once also known as Jug Ken Row) named after their builder and dating from the late 17th and early 18th centuries.

The most-photographed building distinction probably goes to 16th century cottages at 36, 38 and 40 Linkfield Lane, Redhill, with their open aspect. Also attractive, and certainly high profile, is the nearby Red Lion at Linkfield Corner. Reigate Grammar School benefited from the will of Robert Bishop, who died in 1700 and left this building, then a house,

to pay the rent every year, '*to the master who should teach school,*' i.e. to pay towards the living of the master at the Grammar School.

In the vicinity are other houses and structures of some age, including the 18th century Warwick Lodge and a nearby outbuilding made of Reigate stone. Occupying a position on the corner of Linkfield Street and Fengates Road the imposing residence of Fengates House stands on ground that was once a farm called Fengates (previously Ffengatys or Fengaytes) described in old records as being approximately 30 acres. Fengates Farm was once owned by Thomas Blatt, the earliest recorded owner of the Tannery in what was Tannery Lane and is now Oakdene Road, off Linkfield Street. He was a Congregationalist who became a prominent Quaker, and some Quaker meetings were held at Fengates. Among visitors to their meetings was William Penn, who became the founder of Pennsylvania in the USA. Thomas Blatt was given the task of finding alternative accommodation for these meetings; somewhere more convenient and permanent. His endeavours in this respect resulted in a meeting house being erected in 1688 on ground on the Reigate Road near the Grammar School.

The present Fengates House dates from the early 18th century. Old oak roof timbers are perhaps from the original farm building or, as another theory has it, from an old sailing ship. What remained of the farm and its acres was sold off in the 1870s and 80s and developed into the roads and other houses we see in that area today. Elm Road (previously Elms Road) was once a farm track. Thomas Blatt's tanyard in Oakdene Road (formerly Tanyard Lane) has now gone; all that remains is an old 18th century black barn that once was used to store oak bark.

Further up the hill the 16th century White Lion, said to be the oldest building in the area in continuous use as an inn

'Before and After' pictures of the cottages in Linkfield Lane show them not substantially altered over the years. The hedges and ivy have gone, the lower floors nave been rebuilt using painted brick, the upper beams have been exposed, and a well-matching extension has been added.

or public house, does not look its age because of later additions to its structure, but across the road, on the small, grassed area sometimes known as 'Goose Green' after a painting of a girl with geese there, are cottages that seem older but are in fact a century or so younger than the White Lion, being of 18th century origin.

Copyhold cottages by the stream off Cavendish Road are 17th century and there are houses in Common Road dating from the 17th, 18th and 19th centuries. Most buildings we pass every day without taking a great deal of notice of them, but certain ones we expect to be old and of historic interest. The windmill on Wray Common stands out as a prime example, yet its structure and that of the granary building alongside, although they certainly pre-date Redhill, are only of 1824 vintage, not as old as one might expect. There are other places that one would be forgiven for not thinking of as particularly aged. These might include the Hatch public house and nearby buildings which date from the 17th century and were formerly a workhouse.

While on the subject of public houses - the Plough at St John's dates from the 16th century and the Prince Albert (now the Mongolian) is 18th century. The old Rising Sun public house on Whitepost Hill is younger, being 19th century but no longer looks quite like it perhaps once did, now being a private house. Brighton Road has the Firs, formerly the Somers Arms, and the New Inn, both early 19th century.

There are other pre-Redhill buildings. Chilmead Farm in Cormongers Lane, Chart Cottages East in Nutfield Road and the former Royal Philanthropic Offices all date from the 16th century. Buildings from the 17th century exist in Hooley Lane and Mill Street. 18th century structures still stand in some of these roads and others, and early 19th century houses are also around. In Hooley Lane

is an 1839 engine shed by David Mocatta, who is renowned for his railway architecture. He also designed the Redstone Hill railway station building only a few years later. Two houses, Claremont and Belmont, in London Road date from 1830.

The oldest building in Redhill? That distinction probably goes to the appropriately named 'The Old Cottage' in Mill Street, which dates from the 14th century. There are other old buildings in the area, the above is not a comprehensive list, and the Redhill area only is being considered. Include the rest of the Borough of Reigate and there is a great wealth of the past still to be seen. History is never far away.

Gone Forever

Perhaps there are remnants of buildings long gone if we knew where to look - a buried stone step here, a fallen gate post there, an old archway incorporated into a wall - but in the most part the old sites have been redeveloped and nothing at all is left, as modern demolition and land clearance techniques followed by rebuilding leave no traces of the character of what went before.

'Earlswood Mount' once the home of E.C.P.Hull, JP, who gave part of his name to Pendleton Road.

Redstone Manor

Redstone was one of the sub-manors, carved out of the manor of Reigate. When the Manor House was built is uncertain. In his book, *'Reigate, Its Story Through the Ages'*, Wilfrid Hooper relates that when Redstone Manor House was conveyed to John Husee from John Mitchell in 1583 its deed contained one of the earliest references to Fullers Earth when, *'the Fulling Earth Field'* and other land was let for 60 years to one Anthony Gilmin.

Accounts also relate that in 1786 a Mr Christie advertised the Manor House for sale, describing it as an elegant mansion with garden, orchard, and more than 109 acres, and that there were many other owners, including Lord Colebrook of Gatton and Lord Newhaven, and in 1859 Henry Webb resided there.

Redstone Manor was a part of Hooley, one of the five petty boroughs of the Foreign of Reigate. Each of these smaller manors had its own horse pound where stray horses were kept, and Hooley's was in the fork of Redstone Hollow and what is now Philanthropic Road. A picture of it shows the horse pound in the

foreground with Redstone Manor behind it. Clair Grece, the first Town Clerk of the Reigate Council, remembered the pound as a place where vagrants camped and somewhere for others not to linger, especially at night when passing by the spot might be better done with alacrity.

A mile or so away, on the corner of Linkfield Lane and Station Road, once stood another large house that had been built, possibly as early as the first part of the 17th century, as Linkfield Manor House. It is said by R.Phillips, in his 1885 book describing the Borough of Reigate, to have been plain externally but commodious and quaint inside, with most of the rooms panelled.

A name this house acquired locally was 'The Barracks' because sick troops returning from the south coast to London after the Flushing expedition under the Duke of York had it opened to them by its owner. The building fell into disrepair some time after this and became the home of a number of poor labouring families. It was demolished in 1861 and in its place was built the Globe Temperance Hotel, a building that was home to the YMCA for a while. Oxford House, at the top of Oxford Road, was built in its old orchard. Both the Globe and Oxford House are now also gone, the site of the former being the roundabout at Linkfield corner.

Leafy Linkfield Lane and a thatched cottage that once stood there.

Extremely small terraced houses at St John's, long since demolished. An indication of the low build quality was the fact that worms would appear between the tiles of the kitchen floor.

Early Industry

While Reigate was growing from a medieval village into a thriving market town so nearby communities also had individual industries briskly evolving. The Reigate Stone mine at Merstham had supplied stone for use at Windsor Castle in 1360, Henry VIII's chapel at Westminster Abbey in 1395, and would supply stone for the internal filling of the new London Bridge in 1827 and 1830. In the 1970s the motorway almost completely obliterated these quarries.

In 1800 or 1801 George Hall had left Horsham. His father had died six years previously and his mother had been having such a hard time feeding the large Hall family that George felt compelled to leave home to seek work in London. He had to walk there and was seen at Merstham by the Rev. William Jolliffe, who took pity on the weary lad and took him home to find him something to eat. The reverend was managing the Merstham estate at the time and suggested the lad worked in the lime quarry. The offer was accepted and George stayed, became an apprentice, and in 1808 married a local girl. One thing led to another and in 1824 George took a lease on the quarry, thereby becoming his own master. He also became closely connected with the horse-drawn Iron Railway and established the Redhill business of Hall and Co. Ltd.

Between Redhill and Nutfield, in the Manor of Redstone, were the Fulling Earth field and pits, which formed part of Copyhold Farm. The first local references to them seem to be in 1583, although it may have been used considerably earlier as there was certainly a demand for the earth in the Middle Ages. It is also said that Fulling Earth was known to, and worked by, the Romans. Fulling Earth, now usually called Fullers Earth, was sold in the Parish and elsewhere, and by 1809 was being conveyed to London on the Iron Railway. (See p38 for the Iron Railway) The Fullers Earth Union Ltd succeeded individual ownership, followed by Laporte industries. The earth, once used mainly for fulling (cleaning) woollen cloth, is still used for that purpose, although soap is now also used, but its main use is now for refining, de-colouring, and

Before the days of machinery at the Fullers Earth pits

deodorising oils, and provides absorbent materials such as cat litter.

Earlswood Common's Weald clay was used for brick and tile making more or less continuously from the Middle Ages. Brickworks also existed at Cockshot Hill, Holmethorpe, and other local places. At Meadvale the trade was carried on at Brown's Brickyard until the 20th century. The brickworks was where Arbutus, Willow and Hornbeam roads were built in the 1950s.

The lower of the two Earlswood lakes, known as 'New Pond' in spite of being by far the older of the pair, was created by the removal of clay possibly from as early

It is 1928 and a young man poses happily for the camera in Hardwicke Road, Meadvale. To us the main interest in the picture is what lies behind him. The road ends at fields that were in part the local brickworks, whereas today's Hardwicke Road continues into Arbutus Road, and the site of the old workings is covered with houses.

as the 1300s. Medieval pottery kilns probably existed in several places on or near Earlswood Common and early examples of pottery have been found there, including one jug now in Guildford Museum. A kiln was excavated in 1974 at a spot where the Whitebushes housing estate now is.

These activities demonstrate that although Redhill town was not yet in existence local ancient skills were passed down through the generations. The Borough's first Town Clerk related in reminiscences of his that tramps used to cut sticks from hedgerows and coat the tips at both ends with brimstone, thus making a forerunner of today's match, and sold them at a penny a bunch. Such matches would have served to take the place of the tinderbox, by which fire was kindled from flint and steel. Dr Grece was speaking of a time in the 1830's, shortly before the coming of the railway.

The oldest, most extensive and most labour intensive of all industries was that of raising crops and stock. First man alone, then man and ox, later man and horse, toiled and tilled in all weathers for thousands of years to produce the food he needed to live. The story of agriculture is deep in our existence, its history long, but no event was to change its course more than the invention of machinery in the 19th century, revolutionising an industry that had seen little change since the invention of the wheel. During the latter part of the 19th century and the early part of the 20th, thousands of people left the countryside to seek work in the towns and cities of England. Country girls went into service, working for townsfolk for whom the industrial revolution had meant as much prosperity as it had meant hardship and loss of labour opportunities for their new employees. Men worked where they could, in factories, shops, or in service as coachmen and retainers to large households, anywhere where they were able to find employment. Populations of villages shrank, populations of towns grew. Today, instead of gangs of men and women labouring in large fields for days at a time those same fields are visited by a machine, often driven by one man alone, the job completed within hours, the machine moving on to another task elsewhere, leaving the field empty again. Machines not only meant less labour required, they also meant less land needed. With improvements in agricultural techniques and the availability of improved strains of seed, surplus land began to be sold for much needed suburban development. Much of the countryside, previously undisturbed except for the growing and harvesting cycles of centuries, became populated not by hordes of agricultural labourers but by people living in modern housing, people who rarely gave a thought to the fact that where they lived streams had flowed, birds had nested, foxes had foraged and man had worked the soil for generations. Fields our grandfathers tilled on weekdays disappeared under housing estates; woods in which they beat the undergrowth for weekend shooting parties were cleared for roads and motorways.

It is a process that continues. Much of the ground on which Redhill is built was not good farming country, too wet for the purpose - too wet for a town many thought in the early days - but surrounding it were farming areas long since used for non-farming purposes.

Tanning has been a local industry since at least the 14th century. There were three tanneries in the Borough at the beginning of the 19th century, one at Hooley, one at Meadvale and one off Linkfield Street, Redhill, only the latter surviving into living memory. It was in existence in the 17th century, owned then by Thomas Blatt and his son John, who held the copyhold (a method of owning property) from Reigate Manor. It remained in their hands until 1748 when they surrendered that copyhold to John

Baker. In 1800 John Wright took over *'barns, stable, kiln, bark (oak) mill, garden and orchard - 2 acres'*. It was subsequently acquired by John Tosswill who, in 1854, sold it to Ebenezer Hooper. His son, T.R.Hooper, wrote about his father bringing the family to the tannery in Tanyard Lane (now Oakdene Road). This story is looked at in detail later in this history.

In 1864 the tannery was sold to Samuel Barrow, about whom the Victoria History of Surrey 1905 (vol. 2 p339-40) says, *'A very important Bermondsey firm of Tanners is that of Samuel Barrow and Bros. Ltd., started 1848 as John Barrow and Sons. Mr Samuel Barrow purchased a large tannery at Redhill in 1864. Mr S.Barrow still controls the firm.'*

Mr Samuel Barrow became Sir Samuel Barrow and built himself a grand mansion, Lorne House, on the south-west corner of the site at the junction of Oakdene Road and Linkfield Street, possibly at the expense of a house previously on the site.

From 1900 to 1920 the tannery was in the management of Barrow, Hepburn and Gale, during when much was done to mechanise the works. In 1920 the concern was bought by G.A.Bacon - sometime Messrs Bacon and Son - and remained in their hands until 1961 when production was moved to Edenbridge. Reigate Corporation bought the site in 1970 for housing.

Before the railway the raw cowhides arrived by horse and cart from the surrounding farms. When the S.E.Railway built the Redhill-Reading line in 1849 a siding was made into the works and the raw materials came by rail. The tanning process, from cowhide to leather, was a fairly lengthy one, shortened as advances improved its various stages. One of the most noticeable effects of the tannery upon the local area was a pungent smell, not surprising considering the materials and chemicals being used in the various stages of the process.

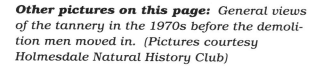

Top Left: *A view east along Oakdene Road, with the Tannery's old boiler chimney on the left and the barn that once held oak bark used in the tanning process on the right.*

Other pictures on this page: *General views of the tannery in the 1970s before the demolition men moved in. (Pictures courtesy Holmesdale Natural History Club)*

Institutions

The Workhouse

The monasteries were the first to look after the poor. When they were dissolved by Henry Vlll hospitals and almshouses were built in London and other parts of the country by public benefactors. In 1601, towards the end of the reign of Elizabeth I, a Poor Law Act instigated a poor rate as a responsibility of the parish, with overseers being appointed for the purpose. In 1631 an attempt to establish local almshouses came to nothing. Legislation in the second half of the 17th century allowed a man to go and work in another parish only if he had a certificate acknowledging his original parish to be his place of permanent settlement. This allowed him to be returned should he apply for relief.

In 1723 another Act sanctioned the building of workhouses, also the responsibility of the parish. The first local workhouse was opened in 1730 in Reigate Borough at the town end of Park Lane, and shortly afterwards another was built in the Foreign on a site at Shaws Corner. Such workhouses provided shelter for the aged, the homeless and the infirm, and employment, where possible, for wages, although inmates were often sub-contracted to others for the purpose of labouring for keep. In 1782 Gilbert's Act was passed, allowing parishes to form together to build workhouses. Reigate Old Borough and Foreign, Horley, Nutfield and Headley formed the Reigate 'Union'. The purpose of the Act was to prevent able bodied persons entering the workhouses to earn better wages than they could outside, and in 1793 Lord Somers granted 10 acres of an area called The Broad Plain near Little London for a new workhouse, and a *'large, fair building'* was erected in 1794.

A Poor Law amendment of 1834 made minor improvements, and two years later an order of His Majesty's Poor Law Commissioners, dated 26th February, 1836, caused the parishes and places of Reigate Borough, Reigate Foreign, Headley, Horley, Nutfield, Merstham, Chaldon, Burstow, Charlwood, Leigh, Betchworth, Buckland, Walton-on-the-Hill, Chipstead and Gatton, to unite in a Board of the Guardians of the Poor. The first meeting was in the committee room of the Redhill workhouse on April 13th, 1836. A Poor Law Commissioner was present, as was Lord Monson, Sir W.G.H.Jolliffe, the Right Hon Henry Goulburn, T. Budgen Esq. and representatives of the parishes. Lord Monson was appointed chairman and Mr Thomas Hart the Younger was appointed clerk, and it was decided to hold weekly meetings at the same venue.

In the early years of the 19th century local doctors took it in turns to provide medical attention a year at a time. The usual minor infections occurred, as did smallpox, venereal diseases and tuberculosis. Malaria may have also been a problem. Little treatment was actually available and most complaints either righted themselves or were fatal. An infirmary was built, probably in 1834, and men and women were strictly segregated therein. A nurse was employed in the men's infirmary in 1840 at a salary of £3 per annum. More nurses were employed the following year. In 1840 new rooms were built for the workhouse and two inmates, a man and a woman, were appointed Master and Mistress of the girls and boys schools respectively, each at a salary of 5s per quarter. Another inmate was appointed porter at 7s per quarter, plus he got a coat provided at the cost of the Union, which showed the respective value placed on the differing jobs. In 1842 there were 232 inmates, two more than authorised.

The workhouse stood behind a high perimeter wall, and buildings at the entrance housed administration facilities. Boys and girls schools separated the children, and blocks separated the young from old and the sexes too, whether married or not. There were workrooms, vegetable plots, pigsties and four wells. By this time the railways had been built and Redhill had become established, the population was rising and vagrancy with it. Vagrants, some with smallpox, were camping on the common.

A woollen industry was set up to provide employment for the inmates but closed in 1847, and in 1854 an infirmary, possibly a replacement for the earlier one, was built at a cost of £1,380. It was not until 1867, however, when a room allowing the separation of people with contagious diseases was built. It may have been here that medical practitioner Dr William Sargeant was employed in 1868.

In 1860 a block was opened to house babies left at the gates and later a house for orphaned teenage girls was added. Piped water was supplied in 1891 but one well was still used in the 1930s. In 1905 children's homes were erected, wards built, and £25,000 worth of other alterations made. The gate lodge was built in 1907 and an extra floor added to the porter's lodge for the gatekeeper. A training school for nurses was established in 1910 and by 1913 it was decided that the old infirmary, with its 41 male, 31 female and three maternity beds, was inadequate. Plans for a new one were shelved until war broke out when the new building, known as Block A, was completed. It almost immediately

became a war hospital, at which Mrs Lemon of Redhill was in charge, receiving an MBE for her work there. After the war the block was returned to the use for which it was originally intended. 1924-26 saw the erection of a new laundry, stores and other improvements.

The inmates, some of them mental defectives, did most of the domestic work. Although the idea had been not to admit those able to earn a living outside, people still turned up looking for temporary accommodation, and the price was money, labour or both. Most of those who had money would bury it outside and dig it up after leaving, a sight that some local residents still remember seeing in the thirties.

The end of the workhouse system began with Neville Chamberlain's Local Government Act of 1929, which empowered local authorities to administer infirmaries. The last meeting of the Board of Guardians was held in the boardroom of the Guardians Institution at Redhill on Wednesday, 26th March, 1930. In 1936 Surrey County Council took over St Anne's in Redhill and the workhouse inmates were transferred there. The 'workhouse' name was dropped and the site was turned into the Redhill County Hospital. The road passing its entrance had its name changed from Union to Pendleton Road.

After the formation of the National Health Service in 1948 the East Surrey Hospital at Whitepost Hill slowly outgrew its site, and by the early 1980s all its functions had been transferred to the County Hospital, which by then had been renamed the General Hospital. It was not long before the New East Surrey Hospital in Three Arch Road was completed and the General Hospital had its own turn at having its facilities transferred to a new site.

Today the site of the General Hospital, and that of the old workhouse before it, is a housing estate.

The Royal Philanthropic Society

The Philanthropic Society was formed in 1788 and among its objectives was the reformation of boys who had been engaged in criminal activities. It began in cottage homes in Hackney but in 1792 transferred to a building at Southwark where it catered for both boys and girls. In 1849 it transferred again, this time to a farm school of 133 acres, later expanded to 350 acres, between Nutfield and Redhill (then Warwick Town).

The Farm School was based on a French scheme pioneered by a M. de Metz. A chapel was built; its foundation stone laid on April 30th, 1849, by Prince Albert; today only its front porch survives.

Two houses for boys and staff, named Queens and Princes, were also built. By 1857 four more houses, Gladstones, Gurneys, Garstons and Waterlands, each holding fifty boys, were built. In the very early days boys at the school fell into three categories. There were those who were accepted at expiration of prison sentences so they could get a new start in life; voluntary cases whose fees were part paid by parents who could not manage them at home; or very young boys who had been sentenced to transportation.

The Reformatory School Act of 1854 made changes that meant that in place of these three categories the school began receiving boys directly from the courts. The work of the Redhill Farm School therefore became that of curing boys who had already entered a life of criminal activity. The numbers of boys at the school rose considerably and at the end of their time there many Victorian era boys were sent to parts of the British Empire. Boys spent their time partly at school and partly at work. The title of the establishment included the words 'Farm School' but the word 'Farm' seems to have been dropped in the 1920s. The basic training for the boys continued to

The Philanthropic School buildings viewed from across the railway, 1851.

be working on the land, however, although in addition to the agricultural labour undertaken by every boy there was, at some time, the introduction of the opportunity to learn a basic trade.

A major event in the calendar was a 'Harvest Home' when the gates were opened to visitors and distinguished guests from near and far. 'Harvest Home' days and Harvest Festivals continued into the 1920s and 30s, probably ceasing at the beginning of, or during, WW2, although the school would have continued to produce food during the war as part of the 'Dig for Victory' campaign. Perhaps the end of the war is a more likely date when the plough started to become slightly less heavily used. This is not to say that the plough and the hay wagon were then unhitched from the horse or tractor for the last time, for in the 1975 report is the statement: - '*Amongst the many facilities available to boys in the school, the farm continues to play an important part.*'

The 1975 report also mentions, however, that the farm had not made a profit for two years.

Why is the School not there now? Reform, or Reformatory, schools had become Approved Schools under the 1933 Children's Act. They were licensed, managed and inspected by the Home Office, and the head had to be approved by the Home Office. A 1969 Act changed Approved Schools into 'Community Homes' with education on the premises. No longer an adjunct of the prison service, these homes, the one at Redhill among them, now housed boys who were placed at the school under care orders instead of approved orders, and who were under the supervision of social workers. Boys were sent to Community Homes until they were 16 or 18 but stayed for periods varying from three months to three years.

Previous regimes had been hard and disciplined but major among the changes was the open door approach

M.de Metz laying the foundation stone of a new school house in 1856.

wherein boys stayed not because they were enclosed within secure walls but because they were a part of a trusting community in which good relations between staff and boys were uppermost. This was achieved at a cost of increased staffing levels, a factor which contributed to the demise of the schools. Another contributory factor was that the personal authority of staff members had been eroded and diminished.

The changes described above actually came into effect at Redhill in 1973, four years after the Act. Part of the Act's effect was to put the control of the school into the hands of a new administrator, chosen from bids made by areas such as Wandsworth, Lambeth and Surrey - Wandsworth's being successful. Although the Philanthropic Society no longer ran the school it was still very much involved in its management, but the resulting structure was heavy and unwieldy. The burden of financial responsibility fell on Wandsworth

Borough, which ran the school as a business with profit in mind, offering places to other areas, such as local counties and London boroughs, at so much per week, aiming to house and educate a boy for less and take the profit. Because the new system was inefficient these profits either did not materialise or were there at first but declined as time passed and costs soared.

Over the years the school had split into three parts: the Classifying School, known as the Assessment Centre from 1973, and which closed in 1986; the Training School, known as the Community Home from 1973, closed in 1983; and the Secure Unit, which became the Intensive Care Unit in 1973, and closed around the same time as the other two units. (Another source gives the closure dates for all these units as 1982). Part of the site is now the home of the Royal National Institute for the Blind.

Harvest Home 1852

Buildings and chapel of the Farm School around 1860.

The interior of the chapel as it once was, airy and light and complete with organ.

The front entrance is all that remains of the chapel today.

(Grateful thanks to Ralph Wycherley for his knowledgeable assistance in this section on the RPS)

The Royal Earlswood Asylum

At an 1847 meeting called by Andrew Reed, a distinction was made between idiots - feeble minded people - and lunatics - those who were insane, and it was decided to set up an institution for the remedial care and education of the former group. An Asylum for Idiots, the first hospital of its kind in England, was set up in 1848 in Highgate, London. By 1850 a larger site was needed and 88 acres were acquired at Earlswood. An architect was appointed and eventually a builder's tender for £29,400 accepted, and in 1853 Albert, Prince Consort, laid the foundation stone. Two years later he returned to officially open the asylum, a stone and red brick building imposing from the front but far less so from the rear.

Queen Victoria's royal charter was conferred on the institution in 1862, hence the 'Royal' being incorporated in its name. There were then 405 patients but in 1869 Edward and Alexandra, Prince and Princess of Wales, laid the foundation stone of an extension for an increase, it is said, to 1000, although it is believed that the maximum was only ever 600. Building was completed in the 1870s and conditions must have been austere for most patients, although there was accommodation with sitting rooms and attendants for those with wealthy families. The sexes were strictly segregated.

Treatment of patients varied over the years. Understanding of their condition and situation required deep commitment to this kind of care, and periods of understaffing, overcrowding and other problems were no doubt as much a hindrance to this process as any other, and it was not until 1913 that it became

The Dining Hall

a legal requirement for local authorities to make provision for this kind of care. Funding, as in most enterprises, can be vulnerable to unexpected crises, and by 1906 £30,000 had been spent on repairs to sinking and bulging walls due to inadequate, or non-existent, foundations, seriously depleting reserves.

The Earlswood Asylum's motto was 'At Last There is Hope'.

One of The Earlswood Asylum's aims was to be as self sufficient as possible. It probably needed to be in the very early days and to this end supplied its kitchens with much of its own produce from a model farm on which some of its inmates were employed. The institution is reported at one time to have had its own water works, and later to have supplied its own electricity from generators. A gas works close by was probably used at one time to supply gas for lighting. Charitable status ceased in 1948 when the Institution became part of the National Health Service. Improvements were carried out, including facilities in the grounds for patients to live together in smaller groups.

Inmates spent their lives there, some committed for trivial reasons, others for undoubted mental incapacity. One of the most publicised inmates, James Pullen, spent 60 years of his life at the Royal Earlswood Asylum, eventually dying there, and his real problem may have been that he was simply deaf and dumb. His fame centres on the wonderful models he made, models which have to be seen to be appreciated. To construct them he first had to make many of the tools required. The Institution had a museum in which much of Pullen's output was housed, but with closure most of the collection was put into store, although some was put on display on the third level of the Belfry shopping centre in Redhill, where it can still been seen.

Welfare in the Community, a policy of moving patients out of the large institutions into smaller units, created the end of the Hospital, announcement of its final closure being made in the national press in February, 1996. Today the site is undergoing redevelopment into a housing estate, with the main building to be adapted for flats.

Into a New Era

The Manor of Reigate in 1800

Since William de Warenne's days his descendants and successors had held title to the Manor, including the land on which Redhill now stands. Those titles passed into the possession of Lord Somers in 1697, and by 1800 it was still the Somers family that was the major landowner in the Manor.

Another substantial landowner was the fourth Lord Monson, who bought Gatton in 1830, the same year he reached 21 years of age and William IV ascended the throne. Lord Monson was to die in 1841, ownership of his estate and further land encompassing much of what is now Redhill passing into the hands of his widow, the Countess Brooke and of Warwick.

In 1800 the Manor still existed very much as it always had since early Norman times, and was divided into two parts. There was the Old Borough, which comprised the 400 acres of Reigate Town, and the 6000 acres, mostly rural, known as the Foreign. The Foreign contained five additional boroughs. These were Colley, which lay north-west of Reigate, the name remaining today in Colley Hill, Colley Lane and Colley Farm; Hooley on the east, the name being preserved in Hooley Lane; Woodhatch to the south; Linkfield, eventually to contain Redhill, its houses then mainly spread along Linkfield Street and Linkfield Lane; and Santon, the lesser known of these names today, almost completely rural and laying to the south-west. There were also various sub-manors such as Redstone and Frenches.

Co-existing with the Manor and having very similar boundaries was the Parish. It also divided itself between the Old Borough of Reigate and the Foreign, having administrative bodies called vestries which met to deal with some civil as well as church matters. They set a rate, a sum which when levied on better-off local citizens was used mainly to alleviate some of the effects of absolute pauperism on the poorest. It also paid for maintenance and winding of the town clock, maintenance of the town prison - the cage - and (after 1809) for men to work the fire engines and to keep them in good order.

Additionally the vestries set rates of pay for those unemployed who were found work digging road stone or the like, and had responsibilities for the poor houses. By the mid 1830s, however, it had become necessary to deal with the poor on a national basis, and elected bodies known as Boards of Guardians took over these latter duties.

The vestries were generally made up of church people and those associated with the church but were democratic in as far as any citizen could attend the monthly and annual meetings, should they so desire.

Bodies organised within each of the boroughs dealt with most other general manorial matters. These included (some) upkeep of the roads, the removal of nuisances, which usually meant objectionable materials dumped in public places, and such other basic matters. Each borough looking after its own was all very well but created certain problems, paramount among these being the lack of cross-boundary co-operation between these separate administrative bodies, of which there were up to seventeen in the Manor overall.

Conditions in 1800 were far from those we are used to today. Piped water and main drainage were facilities non-existent in 1800. Toilets were earth closets, wells were the only source of good water, ditches and soakaways the only drainage. Contamination was a hazard, with disease, epidemics and high infant mortality accepted features of life. Medical men were few and far between, medical knowledge was limited, and communication slow and difficult in a world where smallpox, typhoid, tuberculosis and other diseases, which are either eliminated or controllable today, were commonplace. From many other illnesses, which in the light of present day medicine we accept as not life threatening, people either recovered naturally or died.

The need of the ordinary man and woman to work all hours to scrape a living and raise a family was the harsh reality of life. Pleasures, such as existed, were simple, and whoever was the current Lord of the Manor mattered little. His Lordship might be concerned with higher things, such as getting his cesspit emptied or being aware of just what was happening in Parliament that might affect his wealth or lifestyle, but the ordinary man had no vote, few possessions, and was likely to live, work and die without travelling further in his lifetime than the next village or town.

Fortunately, these conditions have gradually improved up to the present day. Were we to be returned to such a life by some dreadful calamity it is to be wondered how many of us could cope. The events that brought about the changes and led to the development of a second town in the old Manor of Reigate, and how the various administrations were turned into our current form of local government, is what the following parts of this history will reveal.

The Development of the Railways

In 1801, the year of the first census, the enumerator recorded 923 persons living in the 435 acres of Reigate Town in 196 dwellings. Of the adults 184 were in trade and 52 in agriculture. In the much larger Reigate Foreign lived 1,323 persons in 221 homes, this time with the much greater majority in agriculture, and only 50 in trade. Thus we can picture Reigate at the beginning of the nineteenth century as a busy town with a prosperous business community. Around it, at a distance, were other towns, and the rural areas between were dotted with smaller communities.

Merstham was one such community, and by 1806 could lay claim to having the first public railway in the country, even though no passengers were ever carried. This railway, little resembling the railways of today, was a horse-drawn affair stretching from Wandsworth to Merstham. Its first part, from Wandsworth to Croydon, was the Surrey Iron Railway, opened in July of 1803 and the first railway company to be sanctioned by Parliament. Croydon was then the main market town of Surrey, and the river Wandle the most heavily industrialised river in the London area. The railway was built to exploit these industries and to supply London by alternative transport to the road and canal systems already existing. The second part of the railway, the Croydon Merstham and Godstone Railway, was an extension built in 1805/6 from Croydon to the lime pits and stone quarry at Merstham. The quarry had supplied stone for Windsor Castle as early as 1360, for Henry VIII's chapel at Westminster Abbey in 1395, and would supply stone for the internal filling of the new London Bridge in 1827 and 1830.

This railway scheme had begun on paper in the late 1700s and, as its name implies, there had been ideas of extending it to Godstone and far beyond, but they were never to come to fruition.

Part of a bridge carrying Dean Lane over the filled-in cutting of the old Merstham and Godstone Railway at the Happy Eater, between Merstham and Coulsdon

The two railways, joined at Croydon, were owned by separate companies, each responsible to its shareholders. What made the whole a public railway was that anyone could use it as long as they paid the necessary tolls to the owning companies.

Factories along the route had branch lines to their premises, and the SIR's Act made provision for these branches to be up to 1,500 yards long. The engineering work to avoid gradients of more than 1 in 144 on the northern line was minimal, but substantial earthworks were required at Coulsdon and at Hooley where the land rose. There were double tracks most of the way for at least some of the operational years and their gauge was 4' 2". The wagons were of wooden construction with 2' 5" high, twelve-spoked cast iron wheels. They were horse-drawn, although mules and even donkeys might also have been used. A horse was supposed to be able to pull 10 tons up a 1 in 180 gradient, and it was estimated that 10 tons of lime could be pulled from Merstham to Wandsworth in four hours, a speed of around 4mph. Horses did draw much more than this on certain occasions and certainly three wagons might be pulled by one horse. In later years deteriorating track often reduced this to one wagon with a four-ton load. There was a suggestion that steam power should be tried out on the railway but this was never done.

Events overtook the SIR and the CM&G railway companies when trade was lost to the steam powered railway. Eventually all was lost to it when the London and Brighton Railway Company bought all its land for the further development of its own line. The CM&G Company was wound up in July 1839 after 33 years of use.

The Age of Steam

A pamphlet was published in 1823 by William James in which he detailed plans for another horse-drawn line, this time from London to Brighton, and in 1825 the Surrey, Sussex, Hants, Wilts and Somerset Railway Company proposed to build a railway from London to Brighton which would then have continued to Southampton and Bristol. Various plans for a London to Brighton railway were deposited in Parliament in 1833, 1836 and 1837, by which time there were six separate schemes under consideration, with divergent routes and intense rivalry amongst the engineers. By this time steam power had superseded the horse as the motive power for these ventures.

Sir John Rennie's plans were approved in 1837 and the London and Brighton Railway Company was incorporated on July 15th of that year. It was to build a railway from Croydon to Brighton with branches to Shoreham and Lewes. Its capital was in the form of £180,000 in £50 shares. The company had to buy the whole of the now defunct Croydon,

39

Merstham and Godstone Railway, part of the route of which was to be used for the new line.

Plans to route the new railway through Reigate were drawn up but were changed to take it through Reigate Foreign rather than Reigate Old Borough due to opposition from the Reigate townspeople, or more likely one or more large landowners who did not want a railway bisecting their lands. The undertaking was the first major engineering work of John Urpeth Restrick, and work on the northern end of the Merstham tunnel began on 12th July, 1838. The tunnel cost £120,000 to build, and the 3,500 men and 57 horses that were at first employed soon swelled to 6,206 men and 960 horses, aided by five locomotives. Tunnelling through the chalk of the North Downs became one of the largest works in the country, the cutting leading to it being two miles long and 100 feet deep at the start of the tunnel, with sides sloping at a gradient of four in one. At the southern end of the tunnel there was another cutting of a quarter of a mile before the chalk changed to sand.

A section of rail from the Merstham and Godstone Railway preserved at Merstham

The employment of so many workers had its inevitable effect upon the local community, and caused a temporary increase in the population. The Merstham census return of 1831 reveals a population of 713, rising to 1130 in 1841, and falling back to 843 in 1851. The fact that the 1841 census shows less than the 6,000 extra navvy population was due to the fact that most of the work was then complete.

6,000 labourers in the district put a strain on the social order. It is said that there was labour unrest when the workmen complained that the nearest supply of beer, the staple and obligatory thirst quencher, was at Woodmansterne. A strike was averted by boys being paid a halfpenny a journey to fetch the required liquid refreshment.

The route of the line was similar in parts to that of the brook that rises in Merstham, flows through Redhill, and has sometimes been known there as 'Gurney's Brook'. As the brook favoured the easiest path through the lowest lying land so did the railway, unlike the road that had preceded it.

With the completion of the line two stations were opened in the area. One was called Battlebridge Lane, and was situated three-quarters of a mile south of the present Merstham station. The purpose of this station was to serve the travelling needs of the Lord of Gatton Manor. Opened around 1841 the station was closed when the South Eastern Railway Company took over the parts of the London and Brighton Railway in which it had financial interests. The Lord prevailed upon them to re-open it until such time as a new station was built. The 1877 map shows the site to be known as Thornton sidings. In the 1960s there was a small industrial estate on the site, and Wells Nurseries occupied a part of it also. The light industrial development of Wells Place now occupies the site.

The other station was known as 'Redstone Hill and Reigate Road', and was situated a mile further south in Hooley Lane, close to the bridge in that road and almost opposite the Marquis of Granby, now the Marquis and Emperor, public house.

An eye witness account of a part of the actual building of the railway comes from the personal reminiscences of Dr Grece, Redhill and Reigate's first Town Clerk. Dr Grece was born and brought up at Hurst Lodge, Nutfield Road, Redhill. His father was a Fullers Earth extractor and merchant, as well as High Constable for the Reigate Hundred, and his mother was a member of the Constable family of Horley Mill. His boyhood memories went back to before the coming of the railway, which he watched being constructed.

He recalled the building of the bridge that carried the original main Brighton line over Hooley Lane. The railway crossed the road near the brook obliquely and the archway should have been built at the appropriate angle. To save bricks, however, it was decided by the engineer or contractor to build it at right angles, with the result that the pillars of the arch encroached eighteen inches upon the roadway in some places. The road surveyor became aware of the problem when the bridge was nearly complete, and demanded that it be demolished. Naturally the railway people resisted this demand, pointing out that the construction of the railway would be greatly retarded as the bridge was required to carry earth spoil for the building of the line further on.

The railway company was given the choice of either rebuilding the bridge or, as a condition of it being left as it was, to make at their own expense a new straight section of road east of the railway to replace the original angled road, and to replace the ford through the brook with a bridge. In addition they were to lower Whitepost Hill by twelve feet. Although the latter option was by far the more costly of the two it was the one they chose in order to avoid the delay to the advancement of the line that would have otherwise occurred.

The London and Brighton Railway Company first opened their line on 12th July, 1841, as far as Haywards Heath only, no doubt keen to recoup part of their enormous capital outlay. A coach service connected Haywards Heath to Brighton. Four weekday trains ran regularly in each direction. If a coach left Brighton at 7am the occupants could expect to arrive at Haywards Heath at 9am and London Bridge at 11am, a trip of fifty miles in four hours, giving an average speed of twelve and a half miles per hour, no doubt with minimal comfort.

In September, 1841, the remainder of the line was opened and there was at last a direct rail link from London to the coast. Timetables show that the total journey time of a stopping train was around two and a half hours, so the average speed rose to twenty miles per hour. There were also expresses stopping only at Croydon, the average speed of these being thirty-eight miles per hour, so for the first time it had become possible to live in Brighton and work in London.

At first the trains had only five or six carriages, with only first and second class and only first class having glazed windows. Presumably, as the fares were high, the line was used at first for excursions and by gentlemen with occasional business in the City. The cost from 'Redstone Hill and Reigate Road' station to London Bridge was five shillings first class, whilst the second class fare was three shillings and sixpence, not a working man's price. Third class travel was introduced around 1843 but third class passengers were at first relegated to goods trains only, and then to the 9pm one only, which had open wagons. The situation improved slightly when they were allowed on three slow trains a day, but only in anticipation of Gladstone's Act of 1844.

This Act had three main purposes: - to obtain more control of the railways for

Railway workers stand beside an early train at Redhill. The date is said to be 1855, and the man in the bowler hat to be the stationmaster. (Picture Courtesy Surrey Mirror)

the Government, to enable it to purchase the railways outright at a later date, and to increase the comfort of third class passengers. It stipulated that all new lines had to have at least one train each day carrying working class passengers at one penny per mile, and stopping at all stations.

The result of Gladstone's Act was that many railway companies began to provide more than the legal requirements, but continuing high fares gave the newspapers the opportunity to attack the railway companies and make themselves popular with the local residents. The August, 1879, issue of the Mid-Surrey Mirror claimed that the area of Reigate and Redhill contained comparatively few of the city people to whom a penny saved on a train fare was of serious consideration, pointing out that to these people - Merchant Princes it called them - a first class carriage was of more importance than its cost. It added that Reigate and Redhill contained

people to whom the high fares were *'a matter grievous'*. As today, when a company has a near monopoly, complaints tend to be frequent and loud.

Early timetables had to ensure that no Sunday trains ran during church services, but such restrictions were eventually to vanish. The line became busier and busier, and from four weekday trains in each direction each day, making eight in all passing through Redhill in 1841, considerably more than two hundred passed through Redhill Junction in August 1879, according to a newspaper report.

This traffic became the guarantee of Redhill's future prosperity as a 'Railway Town', for unlike other so-called railway towns, Redhill possessed no important workshops. 'Redstone Hill and Reigate Road' had three advantages over some other stations that attributed to its growing importance: -

1. It was allocated the status of a first class station, which meant that it had

more trains calling at it, and

2. due to being approximately halfway between London and Brighton it became a watering and fuelling stage for many of the locomotives, and

3. its geographical location was destined to turn it into a junction, making it an even greater strategic point than it already was.

The Dover Line

In 1836 the South Eastern Railway Company had obtained an Act to build a line from Norwood to Dover, but the authorities decided that the diversion of the lines should be in the district of Reigate (which in the absence of any other town at that time was how the whole of the area, including that where Redhill now stands, was known). An engineer named Cubitt was allocated the task of building a branch line from 'Redstone Hill' through Edenbridge, Tonbridge and Ashford to Dover. Building operations were at their height in 1841 and 1842. The line opened to Tonbridge on 26th of May, 1842, with four trains each way daily, and to Folkestone on 28th June 1843.

The decision to branch this line much further south rather than at Norwood meant that the two companies, the London and Brighton and the South Eastern, had to share lines, which caused animosity between them. As previously mentioned, the South Eastern Railway had had a financial stake in the building of part of the L&B line as far as Redhill. This stake exceeded £30,000, and it afterwards bought outright the line from Stoats Nest to Redhill, the L&B Co. retaining ownership of the line from Norbury to Stoats Nest, with each having powers enabling them to run their trains over each other's lines. They did not share stations at first as the L&B Co. had their already existing 'Redstone Hill and Reigate Road' station south of the junction and, of necessity, the SER

located their station near the site of the junction.

The two stations were connected by a muddy lane, poorly lit, where it was lit at all, and, it is said, negotiated a stream by way of an antiquated bridge. The other way would have been either up Hooley Lane and down the Brighton Road or, if the traveller was on foot, along the railway track itself with a porter to carry the luggage.

(Note: If the bridge referred to is the one in Hooley Lane, which it surely must have been, then what had happened about the Railway Co. having to replace the ford and old bridge there by a new bridge when the road was straightened? Perhaps this had not yet been done - AJM).

The heavyweight local residents, Lords Monson and Earl Somers, wrote to the Railway Times stating that whilst the South Eastern's new station was conveniently situated, the L&B's at Hooley Lane was not. These two gentlemen had sold considerable tracts of land to the two companies, and considering their relative stations in life, no doubt considered that their comfort should be catered for and their opinions taken notice of.

Thus it was that the South Eastern opened discussions for the joint use of the S.E.R.'s Station by both companies, and in 1844 the L&B Railway Co. moved their operations from Hooley Lane to the new station built north of the junction of their respective lines. The new station was known as 'Reigate' (again after the nearest town). The old L&B station in Hooley Lane became at first a goods yard, later a timber yard, and more recently a mini industrial estate. Number 17 Hooley Lane, just across the road, was the old Stationmaster's cottage.

(Thanks to Derek Wickham, whose paper on the development of the railway in Redhill was one of the information sources for this chapter)

Opened on the present site in 1844 and used by both companies, this station was known as 'Reigate' until 1849, then as 'Reigate Junction' until rebuilt in 1858, when the name 'Red Hill Junction' was adopted. It became simply 'Redhill' in 1929.

A tall-funnelled engine steams along the Brighton line in 1857. Geese are tended on Red Hill common against a background containing St John's Church, School and Earlswood asylum.

The Birth of a Town

There is no reason to look further for the source of the name of the new town of Redhill other than the large red sandstone hill that had been known to the Saxons as Redehelde and today is Redhill Common. On a 1799 Reigate map of the area, Redhill Common is shown simply as 'Red Hill', and is similarly marked on other maps made before the town came into being.

The east side of Redhill Common was comprehensively quarried by Lord Somers for sand and stone for many years up to 1883, three thousand loads being taken away annually by rail when that facility had became available. Because of the proximity of this landmark, and the high visibility of the red soil scars of the diggings, it is very simple and easy to assume that the name of Red Hill was a natural choice, lending itself easily and obviously to the rise of a nearby new town. So easy is this assumption that one might be forgiven for being hard pressed to think of an alternative, but in the beginning, and for several years, the name used was not Red Hill but 'Warwick Town'.

What, then, were the circumstances that led to the creation of a new town that was not called Red Hill right away? Why, we may also ask, is the town where it is, in the place that roads once avoided? And why did they avoid it? Was it simply the railway that made Red Hill or were there other contributory factors?

An examination of some of the events preceding the birth of Warwick Town, eventually to become Red Hill, will reveal the answers to these and other questions.

Conditions Change

The area where Redhill now is had previously been avoided by roads for a very good reason - it was wet to the point of being, in parts, very boggy, and has often been referred to as a swamp. The water came in part from the Redhill Brook, which tended to overflow fairly frequently, and other streams crossing the area. There were at least two small streams where the sportsground now is. With poor drainage the ground held water easily and plants associated with boggy conditions abounded, as did associated wild life. Where Redhill crossroads now is was once a good place for a duck shoot.

As roads, railways and buildings have been erected over the years more and more attention has been paid to drainage and the streams have mainly been culverted. As recently as the 1950s the soft ground under Station Road near the station shook noticeably as heavy vehicles passed, and the area between the railway and the Technical College playing fields, now the site of a housing estate, was a fenced-off water meadow full of reeds.

In spite of these marshy conditions, by the early 1840s the area had two major through routes - the 1818 Gatton Point to Povey Cross road and the railway - and the two were not far apart. The railway station was quickly provided with two important accessories, a hotel and decent road access. The first came in the shape of the 'Railway Hotel', now the Lakers; the second was provided for travellers from Nutfield and Bletchingley by the conversion into a road of a farm track down Redstone Hill. For people from Reigate this road was extended past the station via a single-track tunnel to make a

T-junction with the London to Brighton Road. The travelling public could thus come from the west either along Linkfield Lane, turning south down London Road to the road to the station, or travel via Mill Street, turning north down the Brighton Road to the same point.

But some people were not quite satisfied with these two roundabout routes. Thomas Dann, a coal and lime merchant from Reigate, thought that the road down Redstone Hill to the T-junction with the London-Brighton Road could be extended to Linkfield Corner, thus shortening the journey from Reigate to the station. He spoke to Henry Grece (the father of Dr Grece whose memories of the building of the railway in Hooley Lane have already been discussed) and said that he would make representations to the railway company on the matter. These were duly made and had effect. The new road was made in 1843 and became Station Road (West). It was the property of the South Eastern Railway Company and intended for their customers only, so a gate and gatehouse were built near to where Lloyds Bank now is, and only those claiming business at the station were allowed passage. Later the road was left for all to use, although to maintain its private status the gate was closed once a month. The road remained private until adopted by the Borough Council in about 1872.

There was now a cross-roads where once there had been no road at all, surely a classic point around which to centre a new town. Not so, for just as we have already discovered that the new town was not called Red Hill, we shall soon see that it grew up west and slightly north of the crossroads.

Little London

Meanwhile, things had been happening elsewhere. The previously mentioned small but growing community known as 'Little London' probably began as an isolated farming community, its growth at first possibly having something to do with its proximity to the Lord's sand workings, maybe later with the labour force employed on the building of the 1818 London-Brighton road which passed close by. Certainly its population and size was increased by the labourers on the London-Brighton railway of the very early 1840s coming to live there in poor quality houses crammed together and thrown up at short notice.

The people of Reigate were aware of this new community, and some felt a certain sense of responsibility for at least one aspect of its needs. One account summarised the situation like this: - *'The good people of Reigate, having rejected the idea of a main line running through Reigate, now felt obliged to take action.'*

The action referred to was to provide those living at Little London with the bricks and mortar of spiritual guidance. Lord Joliffe, speaking at an 1840 public meeting made a proposition, saying, "*I therefore move that this meeting, being well aware that the Mother Church of the Parish of Reigate is incapable of affording church room for its increasing population, and that consequently a large portion of the Parish is, from the very circumstances of the case, deprived of the benefit resulting from the ministrations of the Church of England, do now call upon the friends of that Church strenuously to exert themselves to provide a remedy for the evil which they so feelingly deplore.*"

Which was a wordy way of saying that a new church needed to be urgently provided for a growing population outside of Reigate.

As previously stated, the Manor and the Parish had similar boundaries. At a meeting of either one or both of the Parish vestries on 21st August, 1840, a Mr W.Price proposed that £411.12s. 6d of Parish funds should be allocated to the building of a new church at Red Hill (showing, as we would expect, that the name was in use for this area at this time). An amendment by a Mr C.J.Smith that £100 of the money be put towards improving the access to the railway station was defeated. Another proposal by one Thomas Burt that the same £100 be put towards the filling in of holes in the waste of the Parish and the building of a gallery in the existing church was also defeated, and Little London got its church three years later in 1843. At first called Red Hill District Church, it was not long before it was consecrated as St John's Church.

Another important matter discussed at that same vestry meeting was that the London, Brighton and South Coast Railway Company should be made to pay compensation to the churchwardens for the loss of rights on the common. The company had bought a great deal of land on which grazing and access rights had once been enjoyed and were now denied. Agreement on this matter resulted, just over four years later on the 17th of October, 1844, in the churchwardens holding a local poll to decide what to do with £535.7s thus obtained.

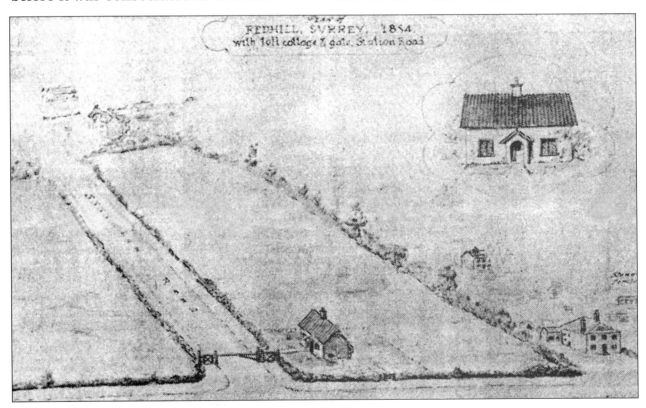

A drawing of the new junction was made in 1854 by Mr T.R.Hooper, who first came to Redhill when his father bought the tannery in what is now Oakdene Road. A copy of that drawing was made by Mr Buckland Kent. Comparison with today's Redhill is possible by the road layout and names. The building in the bottom right hand corner on the London road would seem to be the Queens Arms public house, the writing next to it shows the position of Stenning's timber yard. The building further up Station Road from the toll cottage could be the Warwick Hotel. When the road down Redstone Hill was originally made the station was still at Hooley Lane and the road was for access only, with the old through route via Mill Street, Hooley Lane and Redstone Hollow still in use, which was why the Station tunnel was made so narrow.

The decision was to spend one third on the poor rate and two thirds to erect a national school, and in 1845 a school was built opposite the church. That school, now much larger, and with little or nothing of the original remaining, today exists as St John's School. The name of Little London is consigned to records such as this history, and the area is generally known as St John's.

A Sub-Post Office

Little London was only one of the inhabited areas of the Foreign, not far away Linkfield was another. Linkfield was not a compact area but consisted of houses, businesses and farms spread along Linkfield Street and Linkfield Lane. In 1843 a sub-post office was set up at Mr Comber's house at the top of White-post Hill. It would be easy to assume that this was because of the increasing importance of the area, but the simple truth of the matter is that tenders had been invited for the carrying of the post at night between Reigate and Godstone, and Reigate and Guildford, and Mr Comber won the tender. He already had a building business (he tendered for and won the contract to build St John's Church) and added the new activity to his repertoire. Not that he was too stretched as he did not have to provide a postal delivery service, only the bulk delivery and the opportunity, perhaps not immediately but certainly later, for the locals to post or collect their own mail. How they knew there was any to collect is not clear, but they would have needed to be certain of something waiting for them, as a trip in vain in bad weather along muddy and ill-lit streets could have spoiled anyone's day.

A significant point to be made is that the mail posted at the Whitepost Hill post office was franked with a stamp cut with the name 'Red-Hill' in accordance with the office's location on a part of Red Hill Common. For the first time in a long while things were beginning to happen in the Manor and Parish outside of Reigate Town itself.

Warwick Town

Returning to the subject of the new crossroads, we have seen how much of the land around this junction was far from ideal for the purpose for which we now know it was later to be put. The Redhill Brook, on its way to Earlswood, flowed past the east side of the twenty-five year-old London to Brighton Road at a distance of from two or three hundred yards down to only a few feet in some places, and was subject to flooding. The road drained into the brook and in parts had been built on faggots (bundles of wood) because of the soft ground. The railway embankment, also on the east side, and the rising ground to the west were unaffected.

Ownership of much of this land was divided between the Railway Company, which had bought stretches of ground between the station and the road, and to the Countess Brooke and of Warwick, the widow of the fourth Lord Monson. In 1846 the Countess granted 99 year building leases on blocks of land that stretched eastwards from Linkfield Street to Frenches, and southwards from Gatton to Station Road, and she gave part of her title to name the resultant settlement that subsequently grew up along North Street, Warwick Road and Station Road.

Warwick Town was born.

Public money had been spent on a school and church at Little London but there was to be no more growth there. The situation of the transfer of population growth was, in a way, like that which had occurred at Reigate seven hundred years before, when the church found itself on the outskirts of the town rather than at the potential centre of it. No money had been wasted, however, because St John's Church and School served their original purposes well, and have continued to do so to this day.

St John's Church as originally built. Later sweeping alterations were made.

A Combination of Formative Events

The creation of Warwick Town came about, therefore, through not one but a combination of events - the making of the 1818 road, the sale of land to the railway company, the siting of its station, hotel and subsequent cross-roads, and the leasing of land for building by the Countess of Warwick. This latter was an act which extended part of the Linkfield area into a new growth centre, but there would never have been growth if there had not been a demand for housing, a demand that came from a general population movement and increase, coupled with the new accessibility of the area and the resulting desire and opportunity to service it. Warwick Town also had the advantage of being set in countryside where the air was clean, an attribute attractive to those whose means ran to affording a better life style away from the smoky city whilst being able to return to it on a regular basis. The railway was important, but although its junction had not alone made Warwick Town, it had with other factors undeniably played a major part.

From Warwick Town to Red Hill

From Warwick Town to Red Hill

When the first proposals to build the railway were being put forward Reigate Manor was still in existence, which meant that the land in Reigate Town and Reigate Foreign was still overwhelmingly in the ownership of the Lord of the Manor, Earl Somers, and others. The 111 acres they sold to the railway companies for the laying down of their lines did not simply consist of strips just wide enough for track and no more but of parcels of land that were left with considerable unused acreage after the line was constructed through them.

The railway companies, therefore, had some impact on the pattern of land ownership after their lines were built, as they sold surplus land on to others, but it was private capital that was mainly responsible for completely changing the area.

The 'Railway Excursions Handbook to Brighton', published in 1851, seven years after Reigate Junction station was opened, noted, *'On the Brighton Line you see no human habitations save a few cottages'*. Twenty-five years later the 'Handbook To The Environs of London', published in 1876, observed, *'When Redhill was made a first class station of the Brighton and South East Railways, its convenience of access, and the charm of the scenery, drew to it numerous merchants and men of business who prefer luxury at a moderate distance from the capital. It was of course speedily marked as a quarry by the speculative builder, and on the hill-top has grown up a populous railway town of hideous brick shops and habitations, and around it a belt of ostentatious villas, comfortable looking mansions and tasteful and ornate dwellings of many varieties, with a super abundance of builders' detached and semi-detached malformations'*.

The puzzling reference to 'the hill-top' apart, this piece gives a glimpse of the new town from the outside looking in, as it were, but was it really like that? Is not 'hideous brick shops and habitations' rather too strong a description? For opinions on this subject there are a number of sources to look to. Hooper's chosen words when describing the rise of Redhill in his 1945 book 'Reigate, Its Story Through the Ages', were: - *'The early stages of this building activity, which included the erection of much of Redhill town, coincided unfortunately with one of the most debased periods of English architecture'*.

A piece written by Samuel Palmer, local artist, states, *'Those passing through the ghastly modern town of Redhill, partly a reclaimed swamp, can have no conception of the beauty of some of the scenery not too far distant'*.

Yet another opinion is attributed to a Merstham schoolmaster writing in 1921, *'I think I owe the fact that I have lived all my adult life in villages to the fact that as a child I lived in Redhill. It was a horrid little town, it offered no reason for its existence; nor had it any traditions, or any buildings of dignity and beauty. A crossroads provided an excuse for a hideous Market Hall, a bank which looked like a wing of Dartmoor prison, two streets of mediocre shops, and rows and rows of mean houses; all huddled in a marshy basin'*.

From the foregoing it would seem that we could safely deduce that although the writers were reasonably pleased with the surroundings, they were not in love with the town.

We might also deduce from the dates of the books providing the first two descriptions that somewhere between 1851 and 1876, the original development of Warwick Town somehow changed its name to Red Hill. As Warwick Town had begun its rise in the late 1840s the question arises about how it grew and when its name was changed; if it was a sudden or a gradual change; and why it was changed at all. Certainly the event can be placed after 1849, as in that year a second branch line was built off the London-Brighton line, which turned away to the east, through Reigate and Guildford to Reading. As this provided a station at Reigate that naturally had to be called after that town, the station at (what was to be) Red Hill, only recently itself named 'Reigate', could not retain that title. The new title chosen was 'Reigate Junction' to distinguish between the two, so Red Hill was certainly not a name on everyone's lips in that year. As we discovered in the previous chapter, however, the station was rebuilt and renamed as Red Hill Junction in 1858, so the period in which we now know the change occurred definitely falls between 1849 and 1858.

A word about variation in spelling might not go amiss, as 'Red Hill' and 'Redhill' now both appear in this text. It seems that both forms were used, and therefore both were correct, but precisely when Red Hill became Redhill is not easily definable. In Palgrave's 1860 book, *A Handbook to Reigate,* there are advertisements in which only the forms REDHILL, RED HILL, Red-Hill and Red Hill appear, yet in the index to advertisers the form Redhill is used throughout. It would seem therefore that by this time not only was the name 'Warwick Town' generally a thing of the past but the new name was also subject to change. Once written, a previous form might not alter until whatever it was written on (a sign or

bill heading) was redone. 'Redhill' is the simplest form and it is easy to see why it eventually became the norm. 'Redhill' will generally be used in this text unless 'Red Hill' is more in context.

Early Growth

The original Warwick Town must have been a place of almost continuous building. Those living there from the beginning would have got used to change as vacant plots along North Street and Warwick Road were filled with houses, shops and inns and the skyline continually altered. Development spread into Station Road, with more dwelling houses as well as shops, a public house and a brewery complementing the community with the business and leisure infrastructure it needed, gradually transforming the area and perhaps even beginning the process of draining the wetter, boggier places.

Much of the new housing was designed for poorer families and did little to enhance the ethos of the new town. The air was good, however, as was the situation, being not far from London, and there were wealthier men who saw the opportunities that presented themselves. It was in Warwick Town that R.C.Carrington, the astronomer, who published a catalogue of his mapping of stars in the northern skies of the 1850s, built himself a house on Furze Hill off Warwick Road. He lived there for some years from 1852 when he was about 26 years of age, and his name is remembered in Carrington Close.

Just beyond Station Road West the railway line to Reigate passed close to a brewery. Built by Samuel Relf in 1845 it was in the hands of brewer Henry Reffell, who came there possibly in the early 1850s and who was certainly there from 1861 to 1871. Henry, 50 years of age in 1871, sold out to Cutforth Brothers some time after this year but was there long enough to make his mark, for the railway

*Samuel Relf, builder of the brewery run by
Henry Reffell (Courtesy Reigate
and Banstead Council)*

bridge became known as Reffells Bridge and has remained so ever since. Misspelling of his name resulted in a nameplate being affixed in 1998.

Businesses

The railway station and the hotel alongside had been the first established businesses and were soon followed by a host of others that served the needs of a growing town. Whitmore's Dairy had premises supplying produce from a dairy farm to the north of the town, and the Warwick Hotel was in business serving its customers. Wilkinson's building and decorating business and Padwick's chemist shop, both in Station Road West, were established in 1847 and 49 respectively.

The west side of the High Street was developed in the early 1850s and spread as far as the Royal Oak public house, built between Lower Bridge and Grove

Roads around 1857. On the other corner of Grove Road, on the site that was to become a Temperance Hotel, Joseph Lay had a house and shop

Walter Russell, fancy bread and biscuit baker at 4-5 High Street and Station Road, was also in business in 1850 and was followed in 1852 by the saddle and harness making business of Mr J.T.Sanders. James Rees' estate agency business was established on the corner of Warwick Road and Station Road West in 1851, and with his son, Alfred, he was to be instrumental in much of the subsequent development of the town. His nephew, Leonard P. Rees, a notable chess player of his day, succeeded Alfred.

London Road was also moving with the times, the Queens Arms public house was there by 1849, and other establishments were to follow, but some of the ground was given over to market gardens and remained so for some time.

Warwick Town came within the Parish of St John's, which had been carved out of Reigate's St Mary's Parish when St John's Church had been built in 1843. The Parish stretched from Gatton in the north to Sidlow in the south and was still mainly rural, with the fast growing Warwick Town towards its northern end. The vicar, the Rev. Gosse, in 1848 had a temporary iron church, St Matthew's Chapel-of-Ease, built in Station Road. He put his curate, the Rev. William Kelk, in charge of this sub-Parish and it was the Rev. Kelk who founded the Mechanics Institute in Warwick Road where the Conservative Club now stands. William Kelk died in 1862 and was replaced by the Rev. Henry Brass. St. Matthew's remained part of St John's Parish for a while but the temporary building would be rebuilt in 1866 as the present St Matthew's Church and made a separate ecclesiastical parish in 1867.

Very little ground on the east side of the Brighton Road had been built on at this time, especially above the archway carrying the Reading line, and there were

'Dome House' incorporated a dome shaped observatory from which R.C. Carrington conducted his studies. It was not quite the landmark the present block of flats of the same name which stands on the site is but was still very prominent, and was responsible for the naming of Observatory Road (now Observatory Walk) a little way away on the side of a slope to the east, it being plainly visible from there.

still very few buildings in London Road. Redhill tradesmen came to include William Sanders, who lived where Adams Stores was later established at 78 and 80 Station Road, and who was a grocer with larger premises than a Mr Brown, who had a very small shop in the High Street. There was a Mr Herne, another harness-maker additional to the already mentioned Mr J.T.Sanders; Mr Fowle, a watchmaker; Mr Thomas Lanaway, ironmonger; Mr Oliver Quinton, cabinet maker; Mr Bonny, tailor; Mr Bray, a barber; as well as Mr Lambert and Mr Willet who were both butchers.

Joining these were Mr Miles, fishmonger; Mr Allwork, a chemist who lived opposite St Matthew's Church; Mr Rees and Mr Wesley, builders, and shoemakers Mr Harling and Mr Payne. The medical man was Dr Stone, who became assistant to Dr Martin and Dr Holman of Reigate. In Linkfield Street there was one baker and grocer, Mr Gillham, and one milkman, Mr Vigar, who carried milk for sale in two pails. Mr E.S.Lambert, a tailor, started in business at 5 Station Road, Redhill, in 1857.

As well as the Lakers and Warwick

Hotels other public houses in 1854 included the Royal Oak, the Nutmeg Grater, the Home Cottage, the Queen's Arms and the White Lion. One reference additionally mentions a public house called the King's Arms.

Along part of the west side of the High Street from the crossroads was a deep ditch which was nearly always filled with water. There were no drains and after rain there were frequent floods on the east side of the High Street; the road was often covered with water, and people coming from the station had frequently to walk through water overflowing from the brook. In spite of these drawbacks the town was apparently declared in 1854 Government returns to be the second healthiest place in the Kingdom.

The Change of Name

The main post office remained at Reigate but letters going out of Warwick Town could still be collected and posted at Whitepost Hill sub-office. Warwick Town had grown enough by 1853, however, for this sub-office to become too remote from the town, so Mr Allwork's chemist

'Established, 1849' on a Station Road building in 1999 bears witness to early businesses in Redhill.

MISS MORGAN
STATION ROAD
REDHILL

FANCY REPOSITORY

BOOKSELLER AND STATIONER

A Choice Selection of fancy Work and Materials

Materials for Embroidery and Berlin Work - Fancy Stationery - Views of the Neighbourhood on Note Headings or for Scraps

PERIODICALS REGULARLY SUPPLIED

Registry Office for Servants

shop in Station Road was made an additional sub-post office of Reigate; more convenient for local people.

In order that letters could also be posted there a new franking stamp was made, again bearing the name of Red-Hill to keep the connection with the original sub-PO, but for separate identification it also bore the words 'Station-Rd'.

By 1856 Warwick Town had grown even more and the decision was taken to transfer all of the work at Whitepost Hill to Station Road, the post office in Allwork's shop becoming the only Red Hill post office. If the post was being sent to a Red-Hill post office, the fact that it was at Warwick Town became irrelevant. The name Red Hill became more commonly used and the old name dropped out of use.

Here, then, is the cause of the change of name. Warwick Town, begun in 1846, remained solely Warwick Town for only ten years before the franked name on outgoing letters changed it to Red Hill. The name of Warwick Town faded out and the name Red Hill came more and more into use, and by 1859 several local firms had used the name Red Hill in their titles. Yet R.F.Palgrave, writing in 1860, noted, *'The mass of new buildings seen from Red Hill station is called Warwick Town'*, which would seem to show that the names existed side by side during a transitional period. It may be that Warwick Town remained a confined and separate area for a short while

Examples of Red-Hill postmarks from 1843, 1854, and 1856. (Courtesy Bert Latham).

locally, with its own identity as the rest of the town development left it behind.

Names referring to specific areas, such as Meadvale, South Park, Woodhatch and Earlswood have survived even though their boundaries adjoin others. Although such communities all have fairly well defined limits and are adjacent to other suburbs of Redhill and Reigate their names have managed the years. Warwick Town's did not and, as we have discovered, was long ago consigned to history.

Palgrave's reference to 'Red Hill Station', incidentally, is no doubt merely an association of station with town and not a direct reference of its actual name, which of course was at that time 'Red Hill Junction'.

In spite of the town's growth the area as a whole at this time was still a rural idyll, for Palgrave also wrote, '....by the agency of steam, thousands who would otherwise be now living -- "in populous city pent, Where houses

thick, and sewers annoy the air," gain a far more lasting benefit, from the delectable variety of Fields, Groves, Meadows and Pretty Hills which the Holmesdale here exhibits'.

These words actually referred to Reigate, but to get there the 'agency of steam' from the 'populous city' came via Red Hill Junction which, as we know, was at Warwick Town/Red Hill, and passengers travelling that one station further might have had time to look around themselves. Some, seeing the attractions of the new and developing town could just have decided to go no further. Shops and working class houses lined the central roads but, further away, rising ground provided more attractive surroundings and outlooks for men of means who could afford servants to fetch and carry provisions from the town, and had a carriage to transport him to the station. Large houses were built in Station Road West, London Road, Bridge Road and a number of other (at the time) well-to-do roads in Redhill. Other, even larger premises standing in their own grounds, were built at favoured locations in or close to the two towns.

The Effect on Values in the Area

The Railway Company sold land at various times to raise capital. The sites of many present roads were fields in 1854 but in 1859 the National Freehold Land Society, along with its sister organisation, the British Land Company, bought the land south of Warwick Town between the Brighton Road and Linkfield Street and laid out Bridge Road, Ridgeway Road and Grovehill Road. This land had been bought from the London & Brighton Railway Company as surplus. The company also built Woodlands Road and adjacent roads on Hooley Farm, all now part of Earlswood.

Even in 1854 the price of plots of land

Doods Road. Nevertheless Redhill eventually outstripped Reigate in size, growing to the point where it became continuous as far as Earlswood, with only shrinking common land separating it from Salfords. Merstham, itself to spread at the turn of the century into South Merstham, found itself becoming closer to its new neighbour.

It will come as no surprise to know that there was real money to be made from the sale of land in and around Redhill and Reigate. Values rocketed, in some cases, it is said, from £33 per acre to £1,000 an acre. The coming of the railway caused a minimum four-fold increase in land prices.

Accurate examples of the rapid rise in property prices are not easy to come by. One that has been presented concerns a man who sold a house for £700 and it was resold for £1,200 before being sold back to the man who first sold it for £1,500. This sounds so far removed from good business as not to be acceptable as the truth, but then stranger things have happened, and without the whole story, plus verification, who can say how accurate it is? People do sell houses, regret the sale and re-buy them.

In the second example Robert Phillips, writing in 1885, recounts that a man entered a London auction room in 1858 more from curiosity than from any serious intent of making a purchase. However, a piece of land offered for sale in Redhill was described in such glowing terms that he soon found himself, 'the happy possessor of many acres of sylvan beauty for the moderate sum of £600'. He made the journey from London to admire his purchase but was considerably disillusioned at the sight of it and felt he had bought badly.

So, Phillips continues, he never built his retirement villa there, but he did find that the plot contained Fullers Earth deposits, and over the next four

being sold by the United Land Company for the erection of specific types of buildings, e.g. shops, pubs or houses, had minimum prices attached to them. Plots for terraced houses were priced at £150, for semi-detached £350, for detached houses up to £400, and for public houses up to £500. Some may have been superior plots, each containing room to build several houses per plot, as prices in 1878 for houses along London and Monson Roads were £500 for a detached house and £950 for a pair of semi-detached houses.

Reigate had its development too; the estate of Earl Somers developed Somers Road and other roads west of Reigate, whilst the owners of Doods Farm built years excavation realised him £2,300.

The story does not end there. John Linnell, the portrait and landscape artist, already owned land at the top of Redstone Hill. In his book, 'Blake, Palmer, Linnell & Co., The Life of John Linnell', David Linnell relates that his great-grandfather had bought eleven acres there in 1849. At the time he had been advised not to pay more than £60 per acre but had also been told that there was no land to be had around Reigate for less than £150 per acre and that soon land by Redhill station would increase in value even more. Linnell had thought the land on offer ideal for a landscape artist's villa and so agreed to pay the vendor, Mr Allsop, the asking price of 115 guineas for each of the eleven acres, a total of £1295.

It was thirteen years later, in 1862, when the land of Mr Phillip's account came up for sale. The man who had originally regretted his purchase yet made money from it by the excavation of Fullers Earth, sold the land at public auction to Mr John Linnell for £10,050. Although Linnell's acquisition of thirty-two additional adjoining acres cost him well over £300 per acre he was satisfied with the deal, as was the seller, who made handsome profit and supplied us with a prime example of how the price of land rose in these early years.

In early Redhill the value of the land was probably not immediately recognised. Before the town really started to expand the boggy land in the middle of what was then nowhere was treated as any commodity would be by any trader selling off surplus goods - no reasonable offer was refused. It is said that Mr Lambert, the butcher who once had a shop where Lloyds Bank now stands, related that he bought the land for his shop, plus that alongside where Mr Kennett and Mr Gare had their shops, so cheaply that renting it to someone else for three months recouped his outlay (and it is said that

those who knew him confirmed that he was not the sort to joke about such a matter).

Perhaps even a better bargain was the purchase of the land from Kennett's shop to the Warwick Hotel, if the story related in 1908 that it was bought for £22 is true.

It was also said that there was a time when conditions of bogginess and water-filled ditches alongside the main road put people off buying land, and that some of it was available for £150. In the 1850s this was a considerable sum, but even so, a person buying it at that price at the time could have become very rich.

Over the next thirty years land in the suburbs of the expanding town would have increased in value considerably. Earl Somers and Lord Monson must have had a near monopoly on the land sales; and if there were ever two men who were in the right place at the right time then it was certainly their Lordships. Most of what they did not sell they leased and their successors sold in the next century.

The Story of The Market Hall

The Redhill Market Hall owed its existence, it is said, to a conversation between Mr Henry Fowle, the Redhill watchmaker and jeweller, and Mr Allsopp of Cormongers Farm, Nutfield, on the importance of a marketplace for Redhill. Certainly its conception was brought about by the lack of two important facilities that every 19th century go-ahead town should have, a room for public meetings and an enclosed market.

At a meeting at the Warwick Town infant school in Station Road, on 26th March, 1857, three proposals were put forward. The first, by the Rev. Wynter, was that the growing town needed the provision of public rooms near to the railway junction. The second by Mr. Searle went further, proposing that a market be established and to that end a Market House be built. He added that a committee should be established to form a limited company to raise the necessary capital of £3,000 via 600 shares at £5 each. He named a committee that included Lord Monson, who was to be the first chairman. A proposal by the Rev. Kelk was that the Rt. Hon. Lord Somers, Lord of the Manor of Reigate, be asked to aid the project, and that the high placed persons of the area support the undertaking with a public banquet.

Another meeting, attended by Lord Monson's steward, was held at the Warwick Hotel, and yet another when his Lordship's London solicitors came down. How many meetings in all were held is uncertain, but once Lord Monson (later to become Viscount Oxenbridge) attended in person the Hall and market were assured. His Lordship was president until his death. R.Palgrave, in his 1860 'Handbook to Reigate', wrote about the Redhill Market House Company, *'The company has been established; and the Market House, erected near to the railway junction, will be open to the public shortly. The company is formed under the Limited Liability Act; and the capital will be expended on a calculation that promises to yield a dividend of not less than £5 per cent to the shareholders. Application for shares should be made to the secretary, Mr. A.Ross, Gatton, Reigate; or to the solicitors, Messrs Pattinson and Wigg, 10, Clement's Lane, London, EC'.*

The Hall was erected on a half-acre plot purchased from Mr. Ladbroke (presumably of Frenches) for £200. The architects were I & H Francis of London and the builder was Mr. James Fisher of Reigate. Two cottages had been in progress of erection on the site but the work was stopped by the High Bailiff, who considered the place too boggy to be fit for habitation. This bogginess caused problems with the Hall's foundations and it was always said that the building stood on deep piles. The first brick was laid in July, 1859, but the building was still not complete a year later. The directors were authorised to borrow £1,500 to buy more land and to complete the building. The original cost of £2,002.10s is said to have increased to £3,400, but this may have included the extra land cost. In 1861 rumours that the brand new building was falling down resulted in the architects being called to inspect the roof but they gave it a clean bill of health. The clock that adorned the front of the building for all its life was presented by local tradesman, Mr. Fowle, in 1861, assisted by Lord Monson. The meeting room was

The Market Hall in the 1880s before extensions were added.
The fountain was provided in 1876 at the corner of London and Station Roads.

alternately used with the Public Hall at Reigate for Council meetings, so the Market Hall, apart from being a part of the history of Redhill in itself was the scene of the making of much of the history of the Borough as a whole during the last forty years of 19th century. Council use apart, the building got off to a less than perfect start, for the building's facilities were found to be difficult to let, and the directors had to sell land in 1866 to pay for painting.

The situation was no better by February of 1870, when Mr. William Stenning voiced the opinion that it was a disgrace that the local inhabitants had not come forward to aid the unpaid directors and to assist in the raising of necessary funds, at least part of which was needed to prevent the Hall being closed and falling into the hands of the mortgagees.

Things seemed bad, but a solution was found. Opposite the hall, on the south side of Station Road East, was a large piece of land which, it was thought, could be used as a livestock market while the Hall was used as a corn market. This would resolve the livestock market concept as the company had tried holding a market at the Hall but had found it difficult. The old Market House Company was wound up and a new one, the Market Hall Company, was formed on 29th July, 1871, twelve years and one month after the formation of the original company. New shares were offered to the old shareholders and steps taken to attract new shareholders. £4,000 was obtained in the form of 800 £5 shares. The purchase of the field was negotiated with the railway company by Jeremiah Colman, Mr Waterlow and a Mr Head on behalf of the Market House Company during or shortly after 1871. The land was duly secured, not by the Market Hall Company but by Mr W.B.Waterlow of

The Market Hall with its west wing completed and the fountain (out of view in this picture) moved to a central position

High Trees, who allowed the company to use it as a livestock market and saved them raising a mortgage.

The new company clearly did better than the old one for by 1872 alterations and additions to the building were being considered. In 1874 the capital was increased by £2,000 and the Market Field was bought from Mr Waterlow for £1,500.

The field was fairly boggy and money had to be spent surfacing it. A drinking fountain was provided in 1876, apparently at the personal cost of Mr Robert Field, who later became a director, and it stood outside the hall until the beginning of WW2. A horse trough, also provided by public subscription, was later removed to Shaws Corner and stands there still.

A design for a west wing was submitted in 1878, finished around 1892 and underwritten by the Capital and Counties Bank, which substantiated its backing of the project by moving in to occupy the ground floor. The post office, previously alongside the Sussex Arms in Station Road West since 1856,

also moved into the new wing. On the first floor there was a reading room, library and billiard room for the Literary Institute. Additions included a stage at the western end of the assembly hall, and a gallery to the eastern end. At the north end of the wing was a suite of offices on the ground floor, and above it the new assembly room, which became known as the Small Hall. This had adjacent retiring rooms and became the Redhill County Court, which held monthly sittings.

The livestock market was held on alternate Wednesdays. Stalls were set up for a general market inside the Market Hall until 1896 when the stallholders had to move out because a dance floor was installed. This general market flourished for a short while on Saturday nights in the High Street but later in the year, in co-operation with the Corporation, it was moved into part of the Market Field. The field was about 2 acres in size and oblong in shape. Its surface was irregular and poorly maintained; it was bounded on the east by a boarded fence with a stream on the other side, on the south by a paddock and a private road and on its Station Road and High Street sides by an open paled fence. The fences were fairly new and trees had been planted along the Station Road and High Street boundaries. There were two entrances to the field from the High Street and one centrally positioned in Station Road.

In 1897 it was decided to develop the Station Road and High Street frontages of the Market Field. There were two movements opposed to the change, one wanting the field preserved in its entirety and laid out as pleasure gardens to enhance the centre of the town, the other, perhaps realising that the first option was a lost cause, advocating that the shops be set back and fronted with trees.

The first of these factions was one man, Viscount Oxenbridge, who, at a February directors' meeting expressed his objections, saying that not only would the field become far less suitable

for its purpose but that its openness would be lost to the town and the view spoiled. There was some laughter at this but he persevered by adding that new shops would take business away from the existing town traders, and that cattle being driven to market would block the streets.

Mr S.Brooks, chairman, retorted that the truth was that his Lordship was in a minority of one on this matter for personal reasons. These reasons were not stated but it was revealed that his Lordship had been writing to others to try to obtain their votes against the proposal by stating that it was the scheme of one director, when in fact it was the scheme of all the directors. As far as local traders were concerned, Mr Brooks said that they would get first choice of plots.

A vote was taken and the result was for the development by 170 votes to 78. Those who wanted the buildings set back were not successful either, the shops

The 1904 east wing to the Market Hall was the last big project of the company. It was at this time that the position of the stage and the gallery were reversed to provide for dressing rooms in the space created by the wing, and a staircase was built into it.

were laid out with a service road at their rear as originally intended, purely commercial interests winning the day. Building started in 1899 and attracted Sainsbury's and Nicol's and others to the new development. Nicol's was totally destroyed by fire in its first year of 1901, with two of the assistants losing their lives, but was subsequently rebuilt. In the same year the assembly rooms ceased to be used for Council meetings when the new Municipal Buildings, containing purpose designed Council chambers and offices, were built in Castlefield Road, Reigate.

In Reigate the right to hold markets, or fairs, dated back to the 12th century and in the 17th century Reigate had been one of the four most important market towns in Surrey. The right to hold a monthly market and yearly cattle fair was in addition to the old Tuesday market. Another cattle or horse fair took place annually on 9th December on Reigate Heath. This stock market continued until it expired in 1913, and a pleasure fair held in connection with it at the west end of the High Street expired at the same time. The timing could well have had something to do with declining economic conditions before WW1, but they must have felt the force of the strength of the Redhill stock and corn market. Clearly there was not room for two markets, and Redhill's became the successor to Reigate's long history in that respect.

How much of Reigate's market trade

The Market Hall in the 1920s.
The fountain was replaced in WW2 by a warden's shelter.

was simply transferred to a new venue and how much was generated from new sources is not clear. Probably the transfer was fairly comprehensive and little, if anything, was lost to the market traders themselves. Nevertheless, Reigate's loss must have been Redhill's gain, and the traders who were less mobile, i.e. the shop and tavern keepers, must have counted the cost in the former town, and the extra revenue in the latter.

During WW1 patriotic sales were held at the Market Hall. These were sales of donated items which raised money to provide 'comforts' - cigarettes, gloves, balaclava helmets, socks and the like - for the men at the front. Items on offer in April, 1915, included livestock, horse-drawn mowers, seeds and eggs, a relief map of Jerusalem, a walnut musical whatnot and other such curios. It was a catalogue as varied as the history of the Hall itself.

In 1920 ground still unused at the northern end of the west wing was exchanged with the Corporation for land at the east rear where the old police and fire stations were. This resulted in a two-storey building housing toilets to replace earlier toilets lost when the east wing was built. This building had a magnificent coat of arms of the Corporation on its front. When eventually demolished it was requested by townspeople that this be saved but it seems that nothing was done, and the fate of the coat of arms is unknown.

In 1931 the building of a kitchen, buffet room and a stairway to the balcony completed the additions to the Market Hall, which continued its role as centre of the thriving town. In 1932 improvements costing £7,250 included a new dance floor in both halls, new kitchen with a service and refreshment room over, a new electrical system by Tamplin and Makovski, fireproof exits and reconstruction and re-seating of the gallery, the whole by local architect Mr Vincent Hooper,

The beginning of the demise of the market was some time before WW2, through which time it staggered on. The motor car, van and lorry were replacing the horse, so fewer animals were bought and sold. New and improved methods of packaging, presentation and hygiene of food, especially animal products, took their toll. People, once close to the land and used to seeing animals alive one day and their carcasses hanging in the butchers' shops the next, moved slowly away from such reality and became less used to associating what they ate with what they saw being driven to market. Business picked up for a while shortly after the war but by 1952 it was a thing of the past, the Market Field being sold to the Reigate Corporation. The Market Field building that had once housed animals was divided up and converted into stores and workshops. The houses in Marketfield Road were demolished and the whole area became that bleak testimonial to progress, a car park. After that the company sold the freeholds it owned in Station Road and High Street.

Alfred Smith was an early secretary of the Market Hall Company who became Town Clerk on the death of Clair Grece in 1905. Alfred Simmons was appointed Company Secretary to the Market Hall Company in 1906, dealing with matters of administration until his son, Albert, took over in 1929. Albert's son, Gordon, took over in 1956 and was in post until the early 1980s.

Council meetings had ceased at the Hall by 1901 and for most of the 20th century the rooms were used for other purposes. Of course, politics and local matters were not excluded altogether, public meetings still remained on the agenda, and speeches were given there by many political figures, Mrs Barbara Castle and Sir Geoffrey Howe among them. The Reigate and Redhill Opera Club, Surrey Opera Groups and The East Surrey Operatic Society made good use of the Market Hall, the latter having performed

Alfred Smith
(Courtesy Reigate and Banstead Council)

there; Humphrey Littleton too. In the 1950s and 60s many well known pop groups were booked, the Rolling Stones, when they were up and coming, and The Who are among names mentioned, as is that of Petula Clark. Perhaps future research will make possible a review of this aspect of the Hall's history for vol.2

A circus once appeared in the assembly room on the 1st floor. Those who have memories of it say that there were Shetland ponies used, but have no idea how they were got upstairs. There were bingo sessions and a yearly Music Festival. In its time the Hall saw many varied events, and there must be many stories connected with both the building and the company that could be told, probably enough to fill a book on their own. Eventually 'progress' took its toll and the Market Hall was demolished in 1982, having stood for 120 years.

The busy cross-roads where the hall stood has given way to a pedestrianised town-centre, and the houses that once existed close by have been swept away by the redevelopment of the 1970s and 80s. Although the Market Hall structure is gone its later purposes and traditions remain, with the Harlequin theatre, built on almost the same spot, having taken over as the town's entertainment centre.

there ever since the turn of the century, wartime excepted. Dances were held with local bands, like Charlie Pearce's seven piece, which played to audiences of up to 300. Imported providers of dance music also played there, not forgetting the jazz groups that performed at the Jazz Club, held in the hall regularly in the 1950s. Famous names who played with Monty Sunshine, and who have since formed their own bands, such as Kenny Ball, Chris Barber and Acker Bilk, all appeared

The Market Hall clock after the demolition of the building (Courtesy Reigate and Banstead Council)

This picture of Redhill was taken from the railway station in the mid 1880s before the Market Field was built on. Very few of the buildings visible have survived, St Matthew's Church being perhaps the only one, its spire prominent on the left of the picture. The immediate foreground where the Odeon Cinema was built in 1938 appears to be under cultivation, with the brook separating it from the Market Field.
(Picture courtesy of Pamlim Prints)

Red Hill's Early Years - A Closer Look

Through the description of the events in these pages so far only a small idea of the character of the growing new community and its people can have been established. A better idea of what it must have been like can only be gained from someone who was there at the time, and fortunately there is such a first-hand source that can be called upon to de-fog our impressions of those times with clearer detail. This is the biography of T.R.Hooper, son of Ebenezer Hooper and father of historian Wilfrid Hooper. In 1920 T.R.Hooper began writing his life story, and in its pages are a few invaluable glimpses of Redhill during this formative period.

Mr. Hooper was born in 1845 in Bermondsey, and his earliest recollection, when he was about three years of age, was of the lamp lighter coming round to light the lamps outside his parents' London house. He goes on to relate how, in July of 1854, he was talking with his mother about the pleasures of living in the country when his father came in and got interested in the conversation. The outcome was that his father purchased the tanyard in Tanyard Lane, now Oakdene Road, in Redhill, and they moved that autumn. That casual conversation might seem to have had dramatic results but Mr. Hooper senior apparently already owned a tannery in London, so was staying in the same line of business, and may have had some kind of move already in mind.

Mr. Hooper Junior's biography gives some fascinating glimpses of Redhill at the time. As has been recounted, 1854 is early enough to plant us firmly in the centre of the first phases of the development of the new town, and here are included such abridged extracts as to give a far fuller flavour of the Redhill of those very early years than might otherwise have been possible.

The Journey

'Most of the things were taken by road on my father's van. I and Ebenezer were put in charge of dear Henry Ball, then father's carter. It was a novel experience. Our pleasure was marred late in the day by the fatigue of the poor horse, the van having - by faulty judgement - been loaded beyond his strength. He had hard work and at one steep place could not move the van. A passing carman and Henry, by lashing the horse, tried to torture him to greater exertion. We stood crying in pity. This soon failed, and Henry left us in charge and soon returned with a stout farm horse and a man. This ended the trouble and we soon arrived at our strange new home, and out of the evening darkness into the quaint old kitchen with a turf fire burning in the great chimney corner.'

The Tannery

'The premises....were extensive enough to exceed our expectations. The large garden and adjoining orchard, some parts of which were secluded enough for the Robinson Crusoe pranks of us boys...a paddock with a pond on one side. A large tanhole afforded perennial digging. A bank afforded steeps to climb and gloomy caverns to hide in. The old sheds and tan pits had attractions and mysteries. The house, modernised 50 years before, was much older than it looked. None of us knew that under the newer slate roof was an old sharp

The north side of Station Road West in the 1850s, with the Baptist Chapel almost the only building between the crossroads and the Warwick Hotel. The small building on the left is said to be the forerunner of the Conservative Club in Warwick Road, rebuilt but still on the same site today.

pitched roof that had been tiled and attics sealed off and forgotten. In the large kitchen a tan and turf fire was kept burning mostly night and day...winter was coming on and the dark lanes were awesome after gas lighted streets. Posting a letter after dark was a trial, timidly going up the dark road and stumbling across part of the common, opening a gate and fumbling for the V.R. letterbox in the wall of the old house' [at the top of Whitepost Hill].

Linkfield Street and Immediate Area

'Redhill was entering a new era but Linkfield Street, in which our house stood, was an ancient way leading onto the common and was also the name of a little hamlet - chiefly of picturesque little cottages, a smithy, general shop, inn, a large old house opposite ours called 'Fengates'... let to Mr Barlett, a commercial traveller... and another very fine late XVII century mansion that had become a tenement house and named 'The Barracks.' [This stood at the top of Station Road West roughly where the roundabout close to Reffells Bridge is today]

'Opposite our house was a small farm belonging to C.C.Elgar, of Reigate, who rode over most afternoons on a good horse to see his bailiff, Edward Vigar, a genial farmer from near Copthorne, with an old dame and a family of vigorous sons and daughters, mostly grown up. Stephen Brown, Carter &c., kept the White Lion. Thomas Chapman was the local barber...a little spare man the blacksmith. Henry Reffell kept the Somers Arms and a small brewery adjoining. He had a rather ladylike wife and several children, much our age. Dick Steer, an evil drinking man, managed a small grass farm. Widow Rose, Old Dodd (Master Dodd), Master Fuller, Gaffer Legg, and others whose names I forget dwelt in the old cottages by Linkfield Street. Mr Comber, builder and under-taker, kept the P.O. on Whitepost Hill. He was a portly dignified man, wearing a top hat and speaking with authority on many topics. Just below lived Mr Shelley, erstwhile Steward of Gatton, then road surveyor, a genial well informed man of some antiquarian taste, and a small museum of Roman tiles, flint tools, old coins &c that he had dug up or had bought were in his front room.'

Redhill New Town

'On the way to the railway station, on land leased by Lady Warwick, several new roads had been laid and a number of cottages, shops, etc., built, the collection being called Warwick Town. A few good residences were built or being built near. In one called 'The Dome', on Furze Hill, Mr Carrington, the astronomer, had his observatory and wrote his book, 'Stars, etc., observed from Redhill.'

'In the Station Road, made and belonging to the railway company, was a turnpike gate and cottage where Lloyds bank now stands. The shops were small and unpretentious, mostly kept by people who had immigrated from adjacent villages and towns, the principal draper and grocer shop being a branch of Sanders of Bletchingley. Henry Fowle, a young man of the near two centuries family of watchmakers of Uckfield and East Grinstead, had just set up. Also a Mr Lanaway from Woodhatch.'

Further Afield

'On the slope of the hill, facing the common, was the P.O. in a builder's garden. Beyond that was the lofty expanse of Red Hill - grass, fern and gorse covered and with picturesque circles of fir trees. Half a mile on the further or southern foot of the hill was another small hamlet known as Little London but beginning to assume the name of St John's from the church of that name recently erected there.

'At Meadvale (then called Mead Hole) and South Park, new villages were begun on plots of land recently sold by the British Land Company. Reigate, the old town, seemed to us a long way off.'

Social Classes

'There were two distinct classes, viz. the old inhabitants, very rustic and rural, and the newcomers - gentry, London businessmen and others brought by the new railway to Reigate Junction as the station was then named. The gentry whom I remember were Mr Hanbury, London Road; Mr North and Mr Searle, stockbrokers; Mr Webb, Redstone Manor; Arthur O.Wilkinson and Mr Walters, both of Batts Hill; Mr Symonds, an elderly retired farmer; and George G. Richardson at Garlands. An elderly medical man, Mr Stone, was the only doctor.

'Among the former were my father's workmen who had been with his predecessor, Mr William Toswill: William Kemp, the foreman, Whitmore the carman, George Roffey, head of the limes department - old fashioned, hard workers with much quaint wit and bearing the country title of master. My father's workmen were old-fashioned natives, stolid, quaint and averse to change.

'The rustic boys had contempt for anything or anyone unusual and their gibes and actual interference were sometimes vexatious. I and my brother Eb had coats of imitation skin with fluffy fur outside. It was about the time of the Crimea war and as we passed a group of young rustics near our house the cry began "Here come the Rooshan Bears". This frequent taunt at last provoked Eb to arm himself with a hedge stake and when the ignorant little tormentors began their jeers and pushes he swung it round sharply on the foremost whom were cowed and went off with threats, but the trouble ended.'

This completes the local part of the biography most relevant to this history. These accounts of a Redhill barely into the second half of the 19th century could not be full enough, we could read much, much more were it available, such is the magic of another time - almost another place it seems. Unfortunately there is no more, but there is enough information in these extracts to take us back to far different times than we know of and give something of their feel. Mr Hooper's descriptions of the growing town, the changes occurring at South Park, St John's and Meadvale, and especially of the people he knew, transmit the feeling not just of tremendous change but of the old and the new existing with great contrast side by side. They breathe life into the background of other accounts of the time, and perhaps the sense of movement into some of the old photos, in which a frozen instant of time is not enough to sufficiently impart the reality of life lived by the flicker of candlelight after dark, and little of the personality of those perhaps not-so-long-gone people who posed for them.

Also mentioned are some of the local tradesmen, repeating some names already mentioned in this history. We confirm that Mr Comber, in addition to his building and postal businesses, also ran a funeral business. We discover that Thomas Lanaway came from Woodhatch, that George Sanders' drapers and grocery was a branch of a Bletchingley business, and that Henry Fowle came from a Sussex background.

Other tradesmen (not mentioned in the text) were also local. William Whitmore, milkman and cowkeeper had been born locally, his wife at Merstham, and Henry King, who set up as a butcher in Station Road in the early 1860s was also from Merstham. Others, however, came from further afield - immigrants Mr Hooper calls them - many from London, some from the West Country, some from Suffolk and the Midlands, and in the Red Hill of the 1850s and 60s his ears would have become attuned to a variety of accents mixing with the country burrs of rural Sussex and Surrey.

The foregoing extracts from the autobiography of Mr T.R.Hooper have been reproduced with the kind permission of Mrs Joyce Hooper. The descriptions provided are a historian's delight, and doubling this delight is another opportunity to look at the town through the eyes of someone who was there at a very early time.

Mr and Mrs McMillen

Mr and Mrs McMillen, who lived at 3, Ladbroke Cottages, Redhill, for more than fifty years, came to Redhill on September 13th, 1855, the year after Mr Hooper, when the population was 1,700 and there was a cornfield where Ladbroke Cottages were to be under construction two years later. The couple were interviewed in 1908 and talked about their memories of the town.

Mr McMillen had been a train driver. He started with the North Western Railway Company in 1841, and then moved to the Great Northern Railway Co. The last train he drove for the latter was one from York to London specially chartered for the Duke of Wellington's funeral. Other specials he drove carried the Prince Consort, the ex-Empress Eugenie, Mr Gladstone, and Queen Victoria on two or three occasions.

His final move, fortunately for us, was to the South Eastern Railway Company, and while with this company he was the driver of a train from Reading to Redhill when the engine turned over near Pym's sandpit at Reigate. He was badly shaken but otherwise uninjured. The coaches were zig-zagged behind him and one lady passenger was hurt. He heard the whistle of the 7.20 from Redhill to Reading and walked down the line to stop it, thus averting a serious accident.

Mr and Mrs McMillen remembered that in 1855 there were only a dozen houses in the High Street, and no houses at all in the Brighton Road up to the Firs, then occupied by the Rev. Gosse. The Market Hall was not yet built and the site was a quagmire in need of drainage. The land was then owned by the railway company, who had wanted to erect cottages there but were advised not to as the land was too marshy *(Author's note: An alternative account to the source providing the information on p59 which said it was bought from Mr Labroke).* But marshy land had not stopped common lodging houses being put up in Ladbroke Road just above where the Surrey Mirror offices were later built, and where the land was so wet at times that the occupants were sometimes forced to live upstairs and have supplies put through the bedroom windows.

The McMillens remembered the tollgate by the corner of the High Street and Station Road. They said that there was one postman and one policeman, and the only licensed houses were the Warwick Hotel, the Laker's Hotel, the Royal Oak, the Tower - then a beershop - the Forester's Arms and another small beershop in the London Road.

There were a few shops in Station Road - premises recently acquired by Mr Arthur Knight being a grocer's on one side of the road and a draper's on the other - and St Matthew's Church was then the temporary building on the site where the boys school was built. Opposite was a small butcher's shop with the post office close by.

They remembered, too, the road beyond the bridge at Linkfield Corner being very narrow. There was only one house in Cromwell Road, and Garlands Road was then a grove though which Mrs McMillen said she often walked on her way to the house of Mr Richardson (Garlands) on Whitepost Hill.

Before Ladbroke Cottages were built in 1857 the couple lived in Wellesley (sic) Cottages, and could see right through to Station Road. *(Author's note: Wellesley Cottages not known at the time of writing, although there were Wesley Cottages in Linkfield Lane)*

Where the gas works was built there were three or four old thatched cottages in which an old blind man lived and sold flowers and dealt in chickens. These cottages were subsequently burnt down but the Gas Company's works was not erected until some time after.

In London Road there were four cottages in addition to the beer house. The ground where the cottage hospital was built was an open field and Mrs McMillen recollected gathering violets there. Lambert's baker's shop in the High Street had just been completed, and Chapel Road and other thoroughfares in the district had not been laid out. Some

---

Excerpt from 1882 Street Directory

Ladbroke Cottages *(off Ladbroke Road)*
      1 Medwell Isiah
      2 Fuller Mrs
      3 McMillen John
      4 Jeffery William
      5 Wright Miss

Mr and Mrs McMillen
(Picture Courtesy Surrey Mirror)

gentlemen, including Mr Waterlow, Mr Richardson, Mr Walker and Mr Hanbury, bought the land and erected Ladbroke Cottages. Thirty-one were built, although only nineteen had been put up when the McMillens moved into theirs. Subsequently all of the cottages were acquired by Mr Waterlow.

This concludes another all too short description of old Redhill. History is something viewed at a distance, with years coming between the observer and the observed, but the reminiscences in this chapter have enabled us to move slightly closer to the reality of the times.

One of the aspects of early Warwick Town and Redhill touched upon here has been the abundance of differing origins of the people who came to settle and raise their families there. An excerpt from the 1871 census would look very much like the example shown in the following table. From the children's ages and the place of birth of each family member, it can be

seen that the parents came to Redhill and possibly set up business there at least 14 years before 1871, in 1857 or earlier. Many other excerpts show similar movement of prospective parents from elsewhere to take advantage of the opportunities presented, and to raise their families in the new town.

Station Road, Red Hill				
Name	Age	Style	Occ.	Birth Place
Oliver Quin	42	Head	Cabinet Maker	Suffork
Ann	41	Wife		Suffork
Elizabeth	14	Dghtr	Scholar	Red Hill
Joseph	12	Son	Scholar	Red Hill
Oliver	11	Son	Scholar	Red Hill
Edith	9	Dghtr	Scholar	Red Hill
Herbert	7	Son	Scholar	Red Hill
Alice	5	Dghtr	Scholar	Red Hill
Jessy	3	Dghtr	Scholar	Red Hill
Florence	1	Dghtr	Scholar	Red Hill

Grovehill Road as the McMillens would have known it.

The Movement for Incorporation

From Manor to Municipal Borough

That Redhill had become an established town by 1859 did not mean that all aspects of its existence were perfect. Reigate and Redhill shared the problems of the manorial managerial system of two vestries and numerous uncoordinated bodies within the petty boroughs. Adequate town drainage in the form of an efficient sewage disposal system is something we all take for granted today but because in 1859 each of the petty boroughs looked after its own area, for either town to create a sewage disposal system the co-operation of each of those boroughs would have been required for the laying of pipes across its boundaries. As this kind of co-operation was very difficult to get, nothing had been done.

There were other inadequacies. Reigate had had its own water company from 1859 but its pipes did not extend to Redhill, which had to depend entirely upon wells for its supply. Reigate had had its own gas company since 1839 and some of its streets were lit by this means but again the pipes did not extend to Redhill, where at night darkness reigned.

Most power was in the hands of a few wealthy and landed men who were unaccountable to the population as a whole. From the Parliamentary Borough of Reigate two MPs were for many years sent to represent the 6,000 acres of the Manor in Parliament. These were men who were chosen by the Lord of the Manor and one other large landowner - hardly a democratic practice. The 1832 Reform Act had reduced their number to one but otherwise little had changed. The vote was the privilege of a minority as only male property owners were

enfranchised. This meant that no women at all could vote and the majority of men could be born, live, and work all their lives in the one place without ever having a say in the political scene. Many moneyed people in a position to take advantage of the improved communications had come to live locally for the advantage of the country air, people whose trade was carried on in London. They could vote in both places, with their own interests their only local consideration. They settled not just in Redhill but swelled the population of Reigate and increased its size by building their houses under the lee of Reigate Hill and in other popular areas around the Old Town.

The increase in the local population between 1801 and 1859 caused the structure of trade and society to adjust accordingly. The concept of home ownership being extended down the ladder for people of lesser means was an important development. Estates such as the one developed in the area that would be known as South Park embodied an occupier-owner concept that lead to the setting up in the 1850s of the Holmesdale Building Society. Its purpose was, as today, to lend money for the achievement of home ownership, and one of its early advocates was Thomas Dann, the same man who had first suggested the eastern extension of Station Road.

This rapid growth rate accelerated, and in the decade 1851-61 the population of the Borough doubled again. Improvements in education and road and rail communication, combined with the spread of information through the proliferation and improved distribution of newspapers, created a rising awareness of the political and social change in the country, coupled with an increased interest in public affairs. People were realising that the local political system could be reformed.

Two choices for reform existed. There was the measure which created a closed system of local government that had been adopted in some places whereby a select band of aldermen and councillors were elected for life to a local board by a handful of freemen. There was also the 1835 Municipal Corporations Act, which offered a system with council members re-electable each and every three years.

Great cities such as Birmingham and Manchester had emerged from their manorial control, and whilst the residents of Redhill recognised the differences between those population centres and their own they also recognised that the options available were no different. They were unhappy that their town had not availed itself of the same opportunities. After all, Redhill had grown from nothing into a community, with Reigate, of a population of 10,000, many of which number were realising that their needs were poorly served under the present system.

A public meeting in 1859 began a movement for Reigate Town and Reigate Foreign to become a Municipal Borough. Not all were for reform; those with power - the landowners and moneyed men - wanted to keep that which they had. Those who owned cottages rented to tenants were reluctant to spend money providing drainage, and people who lived in their own houses were just as reluctant to be rated for a system of sewers when they considered their cesspools adequate.

They were more alarmed about the effect on their pockets than they were on the effect on their health. In fact, in the early 1860s a vote on the proposal of improved drainage for the Borough of Linkfield, which included Warwick Town, was defeated, even though 49 funerals in the new district of St Matthew's had fuelled fears for the return of cholera in this country.

The Founders of Borough Status

Parish affairs were regulated by the Parish vestry, held in the infants schoolrooms situated near to where St Matthew's Church now stands. It was here that the Corporation had its birth through the efforts of Thomas Dann, of whom we have spoken twice before, Clair Grece, Mr Fowle and others. The first two named stand out as the prime movers of a campaign to change what one of them, a quarter of a century later, described as, 'an anarchical state of affairs', into a unified scheme of local government suited to the times and to the two growing towns.

Thomas Dann was a Quaker and his business was that of local lime and coal merchant. He had been active in local affairs for some years. Clair Grece was

Thomas Dann
(Courtesy Reigate and Banstead Council)

the son of Henry Grece, fullers earth merchant and High Constable for the Hundred of Reigate, and it was in this year of 1859 that he had started as a solicitor in Station Road.

They were not the only ones who were keen to weld together the Old Borough and the five petty boroughs into one civic entity for the good of all, but it was they who supplied the leadership and energy for the task. This was not something to be dealt with at local level only, approval was required from the highest government office and required the official seal of the Monarch. They had to find out what could be done, work to provide the case to be presented to the authority at Westminster, and mobilise public opinion.

On March 1st, 1859, the Surrey Gazette reported, *'a number of ratepayers of the foreign of Reigate have recently set up an association for the purpose of furthering a reform in the general affairs and management of the parish.'* It added that a meeting had been held at Mr Topliss', High Street, Warwick Town. The meeting for which he provided the venue was in the name of the Parochial Reform Association.

Following this meeting Thomas Dann visited the radical leader, Richard Cobden, who suggested he petition for a Charter of Incorporation for the Parliamentary Borough. Dann then went to Dr Thomas Martin, High Bailiff of Reigate and one of its most influential and respected citizens. He took with him a petition containing the signatures of many responsible townsmen, asking the High Bailiff to convene a public meeting, *'for the purpose of taking into consideration the desirability of taking measures for constituting the Parish of Reigate a Municipal Corporation.'*

Opposition for the proposal would naturally come from those who stood to lose by it. Lord Somers, for example, stood to gain nothing yet lose power and authority. Thomas Martin himself was a manorial officer; if a corporation were to become a reality then his post of Bailiff of that Manor would become obsolete, so he had his position to lose. Nevertheless, in the Surrey Gazette of September 27, 1859, was a report that the High Bailiff, *'with his usual courtesy, fixed the meeting as early as possible, namely, on Thursday last, at half-past 7 p.m.'*

The Surrey Gazette went on to report the details. At the appointed time there was, *'rather a small attendance, but soon after, several of the principal residents of the town entered the room,'* noting, *'those present during the meeting comprised many of the principal tradesmen and influential inhabitants of the Borough.'*

The High Bailiff was voted to the chair and Mr Dann proceeded to state the case for the proposed change. He pointed out that the people of the Borough were not in the position they ought to be with regard to drainage, lighting and many other things that were required for the comfort of the inhabitants of the districts of the Borough, and there appeared to be some difficulty in carrying out such matters as they were then constituted. He said that he had made enquiries and found out that there was one opinion among people of all classes as to the necessity of taking steps to improve matters in these respects, and with the large and increasing population in the Borough something had to be done to get a better system of local government.

The alternatives were either to adopt a system that elected representatives for life, something that had proved very unpopular in the towns where it had been tried, or to petition for an Act of Incorporation (yearly re-elections of one third of the representatives) under the Municipal Corporations Act of 1835 so as to make Reigate a Municipal Borough. Mr Dann had been to see the mayors of Brighton and Folkestone, already municipal corporations, and both had expressed satisfaction with this system.

Born in 1779, Thomas Martin settled in Reigate in 1800 and began what became an extensive medical practice. He was the Bailiff of Reigate from 1811, and in 1859 it fell to him to arrange the first public meeting at which the subject of incorporating Reigate as a Municipal Borough was discussed. (Picture courtesy Surrey Mirror)

Mr Dann then read out the resolution he would propose: -

"That it is desirable that a Charter of Incorporation should be obtained for the Borough of Reigate and that the following petition be presented to the Queen to grant the same: 'To her most Gracious Majesty the Queen, the humble petition of the inhabitants of Reigate in the County of Surrey showeth that the Borough of Reigate and the foreign contain nearly ten thousand inhabitants; that the population is rapidly increasing; and your petitioners pray that Your Majesty will be graciously pleased to grant to them a Charter of Incorporation.'" At a second meeting held two weeks later, in early October, 1859, the Bailiff's place in the chair was taken by the Vicar of Reigate, the Rev J.N.Harrison, who said that he believed the local people to be deeply interested in the matter of incorporation. As a supporter of the proposal he felt that there should be unity of action over the matter, and that it was right that parishioners' money should be expended by people they had elected to represent them.

It took three more years for the incorporation movement to fully develop. In this period it seems that the unity referred to was often lacking, and it is said that Dann was almost single-handedly continuing the process, collecting signatures door to door for the petition to be sent to the Queen. Clair Grece recorded in his memoirs, *'Some signed thinking no harm could be done, and that it might amuse Mr Dann. He was greatly laughed at, but persevered and procured a formidable list of names to his petition; but when it came to the question of presenting it and finding funds to go through with it his backers stood off.'*

In 1860 there had been a counter petition signed by about ninety Reigate residents in favour of the election of permanent representatives. It was sent to the Home Secretary but this was for the old Reigate Borough and the new Wray Park area alone, leaving out Redhill and the rest of the Foreign. This led to an enquiry in 1860 conducted by an official from Whitehall, hearing statements by leading citizens of the time indicating their views on the current sanitation standards. The Rev. Harrison apparently asked that the vicarage should be left out of the drainage system as it was adequately served by cesspools (it was he who had made the reference to unity). Mr Burt, a solicitor, was reported to have stated that after he and his family had suffered from gastric fever attributed to defective drainage he had effected improvements by the installation of cesspools. When the inspector ventured a deprecation of cesspool drainage Mr Burt said that he had acted under a physician's advice.

In May 1860 there was a meeting at the Town Hall. The Surrey Gazette observed that there were, *'some personal observations liberally exchanged between different persons present which do not need to be put on record.'* The paper went on to record a speech by Dr Peter Martin, son and professional partner of Dr Martin, the High Bailiff. He was, it has been said, for the Local Government Act, and therefore against Dann and Co., but he pointed out those local deficiencies that required correction, thereby strengthening the very arguments he was against, so his preference may well have been for the more open system of re-electable councillors. He said, *"The drainage, lighting and other things in Reigate are as bad as it is possible to conceive.*

The drainage is so bad as to be not only excessively dangerous to the health of the inhabitants but in many parts in Wray Park especially, it is inefficient. As a medical man I have no doubt that a great portion of the mortality and sickness in the district during the past two years might have been prevented by greater attention to its sanitary condition." He added that the state of the footpaths had been, *"not only most inconvenient, but positively a disgrace..."*

No doubt there was much further discussion - more likely heated debate if the newspaper reporter's earlier remarks about the mood of the meeting were accurate. Finally the question of whether or not to adopt the system of permanent local representatives went to a poll of the electors. Around 220 were in favour and 320 odd against, which effectively disposed of that issue and

Clair Grece
(Courtesy Reigate and Banstead Council)

left the way open for the more democratic Municipal Corporations Act.

It was at this time that Thomas Dann acquired the active support of Clair Grece and they went together for another talk with Richard Cobden, but he was able to offer them no more assistance and they returned together to carry on with such support as they could muster locally. The 1859 petition was now out of date and they were faced with the task of obtaining signatures all over again.

The local press reported little of the incorporation campaign for a year and a half, but in the spring of 1862 Clair Grece is recorded as having said that the adoption of the Municipal Corporations Act was possible before long. Soon after this the Charter movement regained momentum. New meetings were organised but this time the High Bailiff declined to involve himself with them.

Mr Job Apted presided over a Reigate meeting and emphasised that every householder, high or low, rich or poor, should have one vote and no more; a fairly novel concept in 1862. A proposal by Mr Dann, seconded by Mr Knight, that a petition for the Charter be presented to the Queen, was unanimously approved.

In spite of gathering support for incorporation it soon became clear that the opposition was still active and organising a petition opposing the granting of a Charter. An enquiry originally fixed for January 24th, 1863, was delayed by the death of Lord Monson and the necessity for a by-election. His son, the Hon. W.J. Monson, who had been the MP for Reigate for 5 years, became elevated to the peerage in place of his father and had to give up his Parliamentary seat, which was contested by Mr W.G. Leveson-Gower and Mr Wilkinson. They were granted delay of the enquiry until after the election, which was won by Mr Leveson-Gower by twelve votes. There were allegations of unfair practices, including bribery, apparently the normal pattern of the local political scene at this level in those years. Similar allegations at the 1865 general election brought an end to Reigate Borough's parliamentary status and it never again returned an MP for itself.

In the whole of the Parish there were only 678 votes cast out of a 10,000 population in one 1863 election, hardly any more than signatures on the rival petitions for and against the Charter of Incorporation. This shows how few people were enfranchised at that time.

When the enquiry started it was revealed that the signatures on the rival petitions totalled 153 against incorporation and 484 for; but 12 people had signed both petitions. The main body of votes against came from the businessmen, most of whom resided in the Borough and worked in London, their number supplying almost half of the 'noes' total. Those people who lived and worked in the towns supplied the majority for the 'Ayes'.

Captain Donnelly of the Royal Engineers was the commissioner appointed to supervise the March 14th, 1863, enquiry and report his findings to Her Majesty's Privy Council regarding, '*a petition of the inhabitant householders of the Parliamentary Borough, under the Act praying for a Charter of Incorporation to the said Parliamentary Borough.*' A newspaper reported that several principal inhabitants were present during the day. The commissioner himself noted, however, that, '*a fair amount of interest, judging by their presence, seemed to be taken in the proceedings by all classes of the inhabitants.*'

The case for the petitioners was presented by Mr Merrifield, a counsel of Brighton, instructed by Mr Clair Grece. He dwelt on the strange situation of the Parish that was divided into six parts, each administered separately so that no standardisation of amenities or services existed. He argued that one administrative body would more efficiently and cheaply provide for lighting, nuisance removal, drainage, police, highway main-tenance, etc.

Mr Watkin Williams for the counter petitioners conceded that not only was there much room for improvement in the way the affairs of the Borough were managed but said that it was the most wretched case that he had ever heard when the opposing advocate had said that the man with a cottage had as much interest in the matter as a man with a mansion. He claimed that Reigate's connection with the railway, its proximity to London, and the pureness and salubrity of its air, had contributed to the inducement to men of large means to build their mansions in that town and cause Reigate to become a large and important place. The grant of a Charter would do these gentlemen great injury. It would devalue their property and drive away the inhabitants. The whole of the gentry as a class was opposed to the Charter and in favour of a local board.

The enquiry took several days, with many witnesses called, each highlighting the two contrasting opinions. Mr Watkin Williams' argument says a great deal about the class system of the day. Those who had wealth and power considered themselves naturally behoven to protect both and rightly situated to govern everyone else. Education and the spread of knowledge to the lower classes must have seemed very real threats to their way of life, and the proposed Charter a looming erosion of their position and privileges as power trickled into the hands of those whom they considered to be lesser people.

That this was just how they felt was underlined very strongly in Mr Watkin Williams' final remarks. He said that Mr Dann and Mr Apted were the only persons of any consequence behind the Charter, and that even they were people of small condition. He added that not one of those who had been brought forward for the petition had had 'a good English education'. He claimed the petition had been got up by a parcel of agitators in the Borough merely for the purpose of promoting their own importance, and enabling them to take upon themselves the offices of Mayor and Council-men to advance their own interests and make themselves great men in the Borough. It certainly had not, he ended, been got up for promoting the interests of the Borough.

Mr Merrifield said that he was not going to heap abuse upon anti-Charter supporters. He pointed out that the notion that proper people would not be found to take office was a silly one. He said that there were seventeen separate bodies with jurisdiction in the Parish, and that there were boundary markers everywhere. His closing words were, "It is not a question between the adoption of the Local Government Act and a corporation, but between a corporation and chaos. It would be chaos come again if the Charter of Incorporation were rejected."

Captain (later Sir John) Donnelly's report to the Privy Council was dated May, 1863. He noted that the partial adoption of the Lighting Act meant that a great part of the Parish was without any lighting jurisdiction at all. 'The drainage in some parts of the parish, Redhill for instance, is bad; in some, as in Linkfield, there is none at all.' He drew the conclusion that unifying all the separate jurisdictions into one body would be of great advantage.

On June 5th, 1863, the Surrey Gazette announced that Mr Grece had received a telegraphic message, followed on Sunday by a letter from the Clerk to the Privy Council, that the Lords of the Council had recommended to Her Majesty Queen Victoria that a Charter should be granted. The fight was over.

The Charter was issued dated September 11th. On it was the great seal in green wax always used for the granting of franchises. There were public readings of the Charter in Redhill and Reigate. At Redhill Mr Dann addressed those assembled as brother burgesses, saying that in the history of Reigate this was the first time the word had been properly used. He had had no idea that it would take four years from the date the idea was first mooted to gain the Charter but believed that the undertaking had been carried through in a fair and honourable manner.

Mr Grece did the reading in Reigate in the knowledge that the greatest change to the administration of the area since the arrival of the Normans centuries before had been brought about, and nothing would be the same again. Redhill, once a part of the Manor of Reigate, was now a part of the Municipal Borough of Reigate.

The Royal Charter of September 11th, 1863, incorporating the Municipal Borough of Reigate (Courtesy Surrey Mirror)

The Charter and the First Year

Elections took place on Wednesday 2nd of December, 1863, with Mr. Thomas Dann as Returning Officer. Mr. Clair James Grece conducted the legal matters of the election and new Council until a Town Clerk was appointed. He also had to prepare and make out a list of the Borough's first burgesses - those persons qualified to vote.

The new Borough consisted of two wards, east and west, divided by a boundary line from Sidlow to Wray Lane. Nine councillors were to be appointed for each. When a council was fully established one third of its members would face re-election each year for three years. In the first three year period that third elected with the smallest number of votes would submit to re-election in the first year, the third with the middle numbers of votes would return to the electorate in the second year, and those with the most votes would see out their full three-year period.

Reigate's Old Town Hall, where for generations the voting for Borough MPs had taken place, was where the West Ward votes were cast. In the East Ward the polling stations were in the newly built Market Hall, Redhill, and in the British School, Meadvale.

The results of the elections appear on the following page.

Election of Aldermen

At the first Council assembly in the Town Hall on December 9th, 1863, the first item was the election of aldermen, men with some experience of public office who could guide those without. A number of men had not stood as councillors in the hope that enough support would be elected into the new council to ensure them a position as aldermen. Thomas Dann was one of these.

Aldermen were to be elected for six years, the retirement of half of them taking place every third year in rotation. In the case of this first election the Council was to select which of them would leave office after two years. Heading the poll with 17 votes was Mr George Baker of Holmfels, Bell Street, a middle-aged townsman trained for medicine but turned to city trading, and one of a group who had tried unsuccessfully to establish Reigate as a racing town. Five others were elected with 10 votes each - Thomas Dann, Edward Howard, MD, Joseph Sargant, Henry John Hunt and John Faulkner Mathews.

Henry Austen was the Returning Officer for the election of aldermen, and the above 1860 advertisement was for his drapery business.

BOROUGH OF REIGATE ELECTION RESULTS FOR 1863

		votes
Elected in West Ward for three years:	William Carruthers (note 2)	281
	Charles Charman Elgar	161
	William Forbes	159
for two years:	Richard Killick	157
	William Thornton	152
	Jesse Pym (note 3)	151
for one year:	Dr Constantine Holman	150
	George Frederick Young (note 1)	150
	Henry Austen	150

Not elected: Charles Knight, William Langridge, John Bailey, Joseph Chandler, John Faulkner Mathews, Charles Marriage, Joseph Sargant, John Tolhurst

		votes
Elected in East Ward for three years:	James Searle (note 4)	224
	Edward Lambert, junior (note 5)	209
	Richard Steer	201
for two years:	Henry Boult	196
	Thomas Featherstone	179
	George Weller	178
for one year:	James Mazdon	172
	Juan Henry Fuller	145
	Henry Topliss	136

Not Elected: George Gibson Richardson, Henry John Hunt (note 16), George E Pym, William Williamson, William Thompson, William Roney, Richard Laker (note 12), William Saunders senior (Note 10), Henry Wesley (note 7), Thomas Lanaway (note 8), William Stenning junior (note 13), Alfred John Dulake (note 9), Henry Fowle (note 11), William Gritton, Richard Trower (note 14), Henry Webb, Ebenezer Hooper (note 15), William Richardson (note 6).

Notes:
1. George Frederick Young was the ex-MP who from the beginning had tried to delay the Charter.
2. William Carruthers, a self made builder who had recently completed the erection of St Mark's at Reigate and was soon to start the building of St Matthew's at Redhill.
3. Jesse Pym, prosperous farmer and friend of William Cobbett. His son George stood in the East Ward. He was owner of Pym's sandpit near where Mr McMillen's railway engine overturned (chapter 9).
4. James Searle, grandfather of another Borough freeman, and an active figure of his time.
5. Edward Lambert. There were tailors, as well as mill owners, of this name.
6. William Richardson also stood for election as an Alderman and was again unsuccessful. He became a Councillor in 1864 and an Alderman in 1868.
7. Henry Wesley, builder.
8. Thomas Lanaway, ironmonger.
9. Alfred Dulake, grocer.
10. William Sanders, draper.
11. Henry Fowle, watchmaker.
12. Richard Laker, hotelier.
13. William Stenning, timber merchant. His son of the same name was a philanthropist, became a Borough Freeman and lived into the middle of the next century.
14. Richard Trower, Wiggie, farmer.
15. Ebenezer Hooper, proprietor of Redhill's ancient tannery, religious worker and father and grandfather of local historian T.R.Hooper, whose reminiscences feature in chapter 9.
16. Henry John Hunt, one of the Borough's principal freeholders.

Declarations of loyalty to church and office were made by all councillors and aldermen except Thomas Dann and Councillor Elgar, who were Quakers with a conscientious objection to the taking of oaths. An Act of George the Fourth allowed replacement of reference to God and Christianity by solemn declarations of similar intent to those taken by the others.

Doctor Constantine Holman - a member of the 1863 council
(Picture courtesy Surrey Mirror)

Dr Holman received his medical education in Edinburgh where he graduated MD in 1851, and at Guy's Hospital in London where he obtained a diploma of the Royal College of Surgeons in the same year. He moved to Bell Street, Reigate, in 1852 and later lived at the Barons in Church Street. He was apprenticed to Thomas and Peter Martin and for thirty years was a partner to Drs. Walters and Hallowes. He was one of the founders of the Reigate and Redhill Hospital and involved in many medical and local societies and institutions. Keen on cricket he at one time kept wicket for the Priory Cricket Club. He became a leading member of the medical profession and was knighted in 1904. Upon retirement he left Reigate to live in London. He died in 1910.

Election of Mayor

It was felt by many that Thomas Dann, the man who had done the most to bring about the incorporation into a Borough of the towns of Redhill and Reigate, should be Mayor but there was opposition. The Surrey Journal had said in its report on the reading of the Charter: -

'*Several names have been mentioned as likely to stand for the office of Mayor, and some think Mr Thomas Dann will be unopposed and walk over. If the people of Reigate do their duty, it is very little of the Mayor's chair that Mr Dann will see in 1863.*'

Councillor Young proposed Alderman Baker for Mayor, pointing out that as the Alderman who had received the most votes he could not be said to be unfit for the office of Mayor.

Councillor Carruthers seconded this. He had signed and supported the Charter and had no doubt that without Mr Dann it would not have been attained, but he had since decided that what Mr Dann was doing was not for the good of the Borough but for his own gratification. As a result he stated that he was the first man to go against him, not the stuff with which a good start to the Council's business should have been made.

Councillor Boult agreed that Mr Dann had been the prime mover of the Charter and as such ought to be shown proper gratitude for his actions. He proposed that Alderman Dann be Mayor. Alderman Dr Howard supported this, praising Mr Dann's labours on behalf of the Borough and making the very pertinent point that the Mayor ought to be someone who supported the Charter, not one who was against it. In spite of this Councillor Thornton thought that Mr Dann was still not the person for the job, but Councillor Featherstone countered this by stating, "If fifty men were nominated, there would be no-one more fit than Mr Dann."

The final result was 13 for Mr Dann, 7 for Mr Baker. The Surrey Gazette reported that when this was announced there was, '*much applause in the council chamber, which was taken up by the crowd outside*' (The Surrey Gazette, unlike the Surrey Journal, being pro Dann and incorporation). Mr Dann, after being sportingly congratulated by the unsuccessful Mr Baker thanked his colleagues for the compliment they had paid him. It is reported that both in the chamber and outside he received heartiest congratulations, and upon entering a waiting carriage, was drawn by a number of men to the magistrates clerk's court where the formalities for the installation of the first Mayor of Reigate were duly completed.

When the election of the Mayor was made known the signal was given by Mr William Apted of Fellside, Doods Road, for the firing of a cannon on Castle Hill. This was the signal for the raising of a flag on the Crown Inn, and for the firing of another gun on Park Hill. The news was telegraphed to Redhill where a flag was hoisted at the Market Hall as the signal for more cannon firing. At the Earlswood Asylum flags were displayed and cannons fired.

The New Council

Councillors of today are able to draw upon the experience of those already in office, read standing orders and ask questions of the permanent officers. In 1863 there were no such luxuries. No general procedures or tradition had been established, no experience gained of how each man or faction was likely to react to each other, and there were few men of previous experience to help and advise. Not only that, they were now part of a Council that was divided between pro and anti-charter men, so from the very beginning not all was going to be plain sailing. As already shown, part of the press was less than friendly towards the

new body, and to the new Mayor in particular, allowing publication of direct attacks upon him. For example, the Reigate, Redhill, Dorking and Epsom Journal printed by way of a 'greeting' to the new Mayor a letter to which the initial A.B. was appended. The letter began with such phrases as:

'*... doubtless it is policy to make the best of a bad bargain..... even though the article you have obtained is useless, altogether unfit for the purpose designed ... finding means to get quit of it if unable to make it neither useful nor ornamental. But what is to be done in the case of an article which has forced itself into disagreeable relations with you, and which, unfortunately, you cannot shake off for a whole year?*'
The letter continued:

'*Mr Thomas Dann, Mayor and Alderman! Vanity victorious! Behold it! What a proud achievement for that much abused Quaker! How exultant he must have felt when his friends and followers, with a sort of playful despotism, insisted on drawing him triumphant to his little abode in London Road! How grateful to his ear were the hearty but familiar cheers of 'Tommy Dann Forever!' by which little boys chorused their approval of the proceedings. For this he had fought, undeterred by others' sneers or an exaggerated regard for propriety. Affectionate demonstrations, even from unwashed idlers, may be too much to stand against, and so the new-made Mayor, overpowered by his own feelings and the sympathy of his friends, retired from the scene.*

'*However, we must not be too hard on friend Dann. Bluster and brass are very enviable qualities in their way, although a little troublesome to others.....as his term of office lengthens towards its end, we may come to view the affair as a good successful joke, or perhaps be forced to an admiration of his peculiar mode of supporting the dignity he has*

*won......Has it not demonstrated what
dull pertinacity can accomplish,
forming, one may say, a curious study
for the intelligent enquirer, and an
example for the ungifted ambitious?
We will at any rate hope he will conduct
himself as quietly and respectably as
possible, so that when he next vacates
the office, the reminiscences of the
interval that will have passed will not
prevent a gentleman succeeding him.'*

Free speech was clearly just as free
then as it is today.

Difficult Times for the First Mayor

Mr Clair Grece, the Redhill solicitor who
had been Mr Dann's partner in the
charter campaign, had so far fulfilled the
duties of Town Clerk but a permanent
Town Clerk had to be chosen. It was not
a full-time post; it could be carried out
alongside the normal duties of a
solicitor, with remuneration due for the
use of his offices and his clerical staff.

The pro-charter people wanted Clair
Grece for the job because he was pro-
Borough Council, had been involved with
the Charter from its inception and was
versed in the legal aspects of its
inauguration. The anti-charter faction
wanted Thomas Hart, the son-in-law of
the local historian, Thomas Glover, who
had inherited the Reigate lawyer's
practice from him. Clair Grece was
proposed by Councillor Austen and
seconded by Councillor Lambert.
Councillor Hart was proposed by
Alderman Baker (Thomas Dann's rival for
Mayor) and seconded by Councillor
Searle. Debate was acrimonious but
eventually a vote was taken, the Mayor
voting with the councillors and
aldermen. The result was 12 for Mr
Grece and 12 for Mr Hart.

Alderman Baker confirmed that
Alderman Dann had voted and requested
that the manner of the voting and the
names be minuted. When this was done
the Mayor indicated his intention of

making the casting vote. This meant
that the Mayor voted twice, a procedure
not without its controversy but a
perfectly legal practice which history has
seen repeated. Alderman Baker
suggested that the Mayor should
withdraw his single vote but he declined
and made his casting vote in favour of Mr
Grece. It might not have been an
overwhelming victory but certainly the
effect was decisive, as Mr Grece became
the Borough's first Town Clerk and
remained in the post for over forty years.

Of course, it was ammunition to the
anti-charter papers, one referring to, *'the
very superior man who would have been
elected if all of the councillors had been
of the same stamp as those of the
Western Ward'*. In criticising the new
Town Clerk it described him as, *'young
and untried...quite inexperienced.'* Mr
Hart, on the other hand, was portrayed
as, *'a man who has been amongst you
all his life and devoted much time to
your various public institutions; a
person of integrity and ability, and who
moreover has been accustomed for
many years to analogous duties as the
Magistrates' Clerk.'* The paper ended the
article, *'These two events point to the
conclusion of the utter unfitness of the
Eastern Ward electors for the exercise of
the franchise.'*

Another paper attacked Mayor Dann
directly. Using the proverb about the silk
purse and the sow's ear it declared, *'no
amount of snubs or reproofs can keep
the man in good behaviour'*....crediting
Mr Dann with, *'conceit that is
unmitigated, tremendous and entire'* and
*'dull blind vanity with which his whole
personality seems to be encrusted.'* It
concluded, *'Who could witness his
untimely zeal and disreputable
partisanship'* (in using his casting vote
for Clair Grece) *'and not feel ashamed
that such a man was entitled to write
himself Mayor of Reigate? Is his
inordinate vanity proof against his well-
intentioned ridicule? Has he no*

intelligent friend to counsel him, to point out to him the ways of propriety, and to impress upon his mind the conviction that he should, for the sake of his own reputation, keep as quiet and as much at home as possible?'

There is no doubt that for centuries the mass of people had been ignorant of local and national affairs and had been exploited by those with wealth and position. Ninety per cent of the wealth of the country was owned by a ten per cent minority that wanted to keep it that way, and although there were those who resented the rise of Redhill from nothing to a claim for equality there was no doubt that change was inevitable. The opponents of change might have had some of the press on their side but ironically it had been the spread of information via the newspapers, many Liberal in outlook, that had been partly responsible for the new ways that were upon them. In 1855 and 1861 the 'Tax on Knowledge' (the stamp duties on newspapers and the customs and excise duties on paper) had been removed, and in these years the proliferation of newspapers amongst a population who could understand the newly spreading information was considerable.

Between 1847 and 1868 the Tories had lost six consecutive general elections, with coalitions of other groups keeping them out of office. It was against the background of a rise of middle class political awareness from the 1840s that the grip the wealthy and influential had on the country was slipping. As we see, the grip of those who thought they were the ruling class of Reigate, and ought to control the new Borough Council, had also slipped.

It will not have escaped the reader's notice that the rivalry between the pro and anti-charter factions was divided between Western Ward (Reigate) and Eastern Ward (Redhill) people. It is a fact that people who see differences between themselves and others do form antagonisms and try to score over one another whenever they can.

The reasons behind such feelings, power, wealth, control, perceived importance and others, have already been discussed and were made plain at the public enquiry of 1863. The fact that one of the results of that enquiry was to draw a physical division between the two towns in the form of the ward boundary did not help, and there were many contentious issues to be debated that would fail to improve the situation during Council sessions of the coming decades.

Council meetings were held alternately at Reigate, in the Public Hall, and at Redhill at the Market Hall. This history contains much information from press reports of the time. Since then there has been made an 'Admission of the Press Act', which regulates the attendance of the press at such meetings, but in February 1864 Councillor Steer introduced a regulation, *'that at all meetings of the Council the reporters of the public press have free ingress to take any notes they think proper of the proceedings.'* Councillor Searle considered this too liberal and moved an amendment vesting the power to grant entry to the press in the Mayor. In the event a compromise motion adding to Councillor Steer's motion the phrase, *'until the Council shall otherwise determine'* was unanimously adopted.

The press was obviously satisfied enough with the liveliness of debate to turn up at every meeting, fortunately for us. Not that every meeting was taken up with personal wrangling, indeed much work was got through and the business of the Council carried out in a proper manner. Standing orders had now been completed by the few, adopted by the majority, and all were bound by them, although councillors grumbled about them and there did not seem to be one that prevented verbal attacks upon the Mayor nor, thankfully, defence of him.

The Local Government Act

The movement for incorporation had been strongly based on the fact that, as Thomas Dann had put it, the Borough was not in the position it should be with regard to drainage and lighting. The Local Government Act could be adopted to create the powers to repair roads and improve other amenities such as drainage. So far it had not been adopted in Reigate and Redhill, and the subject of the Act came up when the Mayor charged Councillor Searle with having intimated that he (Dann) had used his influence to prevent its adoption, something the Councillor denied, saying that he did not know the Mayor had such influence. In the same discussion Councillor Boult moved that the Council make representations to the Home Secretary over the state of the Borough's roads, pointing out that in the absence of the Act they were doing very little. In April 1864 Alderman Mathews proposed that the Act be adopted. At a special meeting in May 1864, Councillor Young put forward a similar proposal, saying that the sanitation in the area was 'dangerous and disgraceful'.

If the basis for the adoption of the Charter of Incorporation had greatly been to remedy some of the problems that the divided old boroughs could not or would not remedy, one would think that these matters would have been put in hand with great speed. Perhaps the adoption of the act *was* opposed by Dann and his supporters. The reason for this apparent reversal of intentions could have been to do with the expenditure involved. The rate would have to have been set at a level at which the necessary work could have been afforded, and to do so at such an early stage would possibly not have been political good sense. Indeed, Councillor Steer opposed the motion on the grounds of the cost involved, saying that a

Wells were once the only source of water in Redhill, and understandably the focus of neighbourly discourse.

question frequently asked by those coming to live in the Borough was, "Are the rates high?" Councillor Carruthers, a builder, said that he would rather have the drains good and the rates high than the other way around - probably his pocket would have withstood such a situation - but the resolution fell.

In June, Councillor Young got the resolution passed but failed to acquire the necessary two thirds majority. The following month the Mayor announced that at a meeting of the inhabitants a majority requisitioned the Council to adopt the Act, and accordingly he moved that this should be done. It was, however, to be two years before the Act was finally adopted and the Corporation committed itself to the comprehensive scheme of town drainage, a scheme that had been outlined in the Privy Council Commissioner's report of 1863.

In the meantime, as the new Corporation had superseded the old Manorial authority, it sought to recover from it anything that was rightly transferable. The clerk of the Lighting Inspectors of Santon and Wray Park districts handed over papers and cheques, and the late Inspector for Hooley and Reigate Old Borough was approached for records and balances from those districts. Whether all records and monies were recovered successfully is uncertain.

The Mayor and The Borough Bench

In 1863 there already existed a Bench of Justices sitting monthly at the Old Reigate Town Hall. The Municipal Corporations Act of 1835 conferred upon the Mayor of a Corporation the position of Chief Magistrate concerning matters arising within the Borough, but when Mayor Dann tried to take his place at the first sitting after his election he met opposition.

Mr Dann recounted that Magistrate Mr Robert Clutton of Hartswood called upon him to ask if he really claimed precedence over Chief Magistrate Sir William Jolliffe. Mr Dann affirmed that he did, adding that not only did the burgesses expect him to make the claim to secure the privileges to which they were entitled but his successors might consider it a dereliction of his duty if he did not try to obtain that privilege.

Mr Dann said that Sir William Jolliffe of Merstham had a letter from the Clerk of the Peace to the Justices, Mr Greig, stating that the Mayor, 'cannot under any circumstances be permitted to take his seat and act with the Reigate County Bench, nor can anyone unless his name is on the Commission of the Peace for the county. The jurisdiction of the Mayor of a Borough and that of the county magistrates are essentially different.' Even though Mr Dann produced the Act of Parliament empowering the magistrates to act with the Mayor his argument did not prevail. He tried again when a decidedly Borough case arose but as Sir William had continued to resist Mr Dann had withdrawn.

As was to be expected, the unfriendly Journal published its usual account of the incident, referring as usual to the 'gentlemen' who triumphed over the Mayor. 'Of one thing there can be no doubt,' it said. ' Reigate will become notorious; anything more ineffably silly than the scene that took place here at the Town Hall on Monday last is difficult to imagine. Our representative (?) man, after putting himself in a false position, and being put down in a most courteous manner by an undoubted gentleman, 'acts under advice' and again jumps up to be severely censured by the same person. Such conduct would be unseemly anywhere; it was deplorably so in a court of justice.'

A proposition was on the Council agenda at the end of January, 1864, to petition the Crown on the matter. Mayor Dann assured the meeting that he had done all he could to sustain the dignity, honour and position of both Borough and County. Alderman Mathews felt that the Mayor had been in the wrong and the court in the right, saying that his action was 'very lowering' to the Council. The Town Clerk was also the subject of aldermanic reproof after he read a statement that, according to a statute of William IV, the opposite was true, e.g. the Mayor had been right and the court wrong, Alderman Baker saying that he was sorry the Mayor had called upon the Town Clerk to expose himself in this way. Of the Town Clerk's statement he said; "Such a composition is one of the most monstrous things in the world. If we are to have a gentleman as Town Clerk who is so ready to put us into trouble, setting forth opinions so opposite to such a recognised authority as the Clerk of the Peace, we shall be flooded by the troublesome waves, not knowing where to rest." The resolution was passed and those opposing the Mayoral right to a seat on the bench went to the Home Secretary, Sir George Grey. To their delight he confirmed the opinion of the Clerk of the Peace.

Dann and Grece were not satisfied, however, and also wrote to London. Their reply was different. They received a letter from Sir George Grey, with a copy to Sir William Jolliffe, referring to an Act of Queen Victoria's reign, *'which seems to show by necessary implication that the Mayor of a Borough in which County Magistrates have a concurrent jurisdiction to the Borough Magistrates as to matters arising within the Borough has a right to preside over the justices of the county when they are acting in relation to such matters. I have to express regret that in the great pressure of business that existed at the time the Act was overlooked.'* This letter was read at the next meeting, when Town Clerk Grece heard Alderman Searle acknowledge, "It only shows that Mr Grece's opinion was not so monstrous."

On March 11th, 1864, a local paper carried, under the heading Borough Bench, a report of the first case in which the Mayor of Reigate, Alderman Thomas Dann, handed down a sentence. It was the case of a man who had been stealing from the refreshment room of the station. Mr Dann sent him for three months in prison.

Mayoral Salary

On September 21st, 1864, Councillor Boult moved that a salary of £50 be paid to the person filling the office of Mayor. The motion was recorded as having been 'resolved in the affirmative.' All properly done, it would seem, but it was alleged that the matter had been raised after some of the members and all of the press had left, believing that all business had been concluded, only nine members remaining.

The opponents of Thomas Dann reacted accordingly. A special meeting was demanded by a requisition signed by Alderman Baker, Councillors Forbes, Thornton, Elgar, Carruthers and Holman. At this meeting it was moved that the salary awarded at the quarterly meeting should be confirmed. Against were those who had signed the requisition plus Alderman Hunt and Councillors Killick and Young, making nine in all.

For confirmation were Councillor Searle (Dann's frequent critic), Alderman Mathews, Dr Howard, Councillors Boult, Pym, Austen and others, a total of twelve. The salary was therefore confirmed. In the unfriendly 'Journal' Dann was charged with, *'having done more to bring the Borough into disrepute than could have been conceived to be possible'.*

He had, *'a conceit in his own abilities for which no one else gives him credit, and a vaulting ambition to be that for which he is not fitted. This year in office has been marked by unseemly squabbles in the meetings of the Council - squabbles which have caused the Corporation to be looked on with* contempt by surrounding towns, and the respectable men of the Council to regret their connection with it.'

As usual the friendly section of the press countered, and in the lower corridor of the Town Hall in Castlefield Road hangs a framed document headed 'The Mayor of Reigate and his Year of Office'. It is a reprint from the Surrey Gazette of November 4th, 1864, firstly of an article on Mr Thomas Dann's year of Mayoralty, secondly of a report of a public meeting in the Town Hall at which, as retiring Mayor, he gave an account of his stewardship for the year. This account he prefaced with a reference to the way in which a section of the local press had treated him - 'most extra-ordinary, most uncourteous, most unhandsome.' The Gazette used stronger language, talking of, 'unscrupulous personal attacks' - 'grossness and vulgarity' - 'gross and virulent abuse'. It hoped that the new Mayor would have an easier task and a different reception than Mr Dann.

The anti-Dann Journal was not impressed. In its issue following the municipal elections of November 1st, 1864, it published under the heading, 'The Last of Mr Dann', another, albeit parting, attack. Of the year, it claimed it had been one of, 'humiliation through which we have passed.' Mr Dann and his friends were people whom, 'not even their sincerest admirers would venture to accredit them with much mental excellence, much grace of manner or dignity of character.' Mr Dann himself was, 'in the popular acceptation of the word, a 'character.' No one would presume to say he was remarkable for his dignity - indeed, nature had been in every way niggardly in her gifts to him - but in his own estimation he is a man who will give the stamp to the time in which it has pleased heaven to permit him to flourish.'

He (Mr Dann) reminded the writer of the article of, 'Mrs Poyser's cock (in Adam Bede) who thought the sun got up

every morning to hear him crow. Mr Dann has long since ceased to amuse us; we are tired of him. For nearly twelve months Reigate has endured him and a renewal of the affliction would be unendurable.'

Perhaps the truth of the matter was expressed at the meeting that elected Councillor James Searle as the second Mayor, Mr Dann having cast his vote for Mr Searle. Mr Featherstone said that there had been two classes in the new Council that had been constantly ranged on opposite sides. The Mayor would have been an extraordinary man if he had been able to manage both parties, and under the circumstances had done extremely well.

In reply the outgoing Mayor confessed to having occasionally felt that he had had a very difficult task to perform in endeavouring to conduct the business of the Council in a proper manner consistent with the principals of their standing orders. He said, "Sometimes I have felt it necessary to deviate to a certain extent from the course prescribed by those orders, with a view to meeting the wishes of the majority of the Council." He also said that he had expected the first year to present difficulties, adding; "I hope that the present Mayor's year of office will be a less difficult one, and as the Council have now become pretty well acquainted with their duties there will be greater harmony of action than hitherto."

The Gazette hoped that such harmony would be realised, as would unity, reflecting honour upon the Council and advantage to the burgesses.

Looking back through the years it is difficult to assess the absolute truth of all that occurred, and much more occurred than is recorded in this brief chapter. Nevertheless, although Mr Dann's year, the first full year of the Borough Council of Redhill and Reigate, was over, his place in our local history as the first Mayor of the Borough of Reigate is firmly assured.

Churches and Chapels

*R*edhill has not the years to have churches of great age but there are centuries old churches not far away. St Andrew's at Gatton is probably of Norman construction with the possibility of a Saxon church at or near the site previously. St. Katherine's at Merstham dates from the 13th century and St Mary's at Reigate is probably of Saxon origin.

Religion in Warwick Town and early Redhill lacked purpose-built venues for its expression. People used barns, sheds, front and back rooms, lofts, stables and the like to worship together according to their faith before they gradually provided themselves with more appropriate places of worship. The following is an attempt to bring together the history of the development of the majority of the churches and chapels in Redhill.

St John the Evangelist

Built in 1843, St John's is the earliest of the Redhill churches. Prior to this time the whole of the Manor of Reigate had been effectively within the Parish of Reigate, with St. Mary's the only church. One of the minor population centres in the Manor, a small colony of cottages that had been erected from time to time, was Little London, a name generally used ironically to describe small settlements of unregulated growth on common land outside a town. It was because of the uncontrolled growth, caused partly by workers on the London-Brighton railway settling there and swelling the population, that the site was chosen. Whether anyone at the time thought that with further growth the area might become the centre of a new town is unknown, but

some of the people of Reigate felt that there was sufficient need to serve the spiritual well-being of the people there with the provision of a new church.

When the sum of £411.12.6 was paid in 1840 by the London and Brighton Railway Company as compensation for the loss of common rights on land bought by it, a Mr W.Price proposed at a vestry meeting of 21st August that the sum be put towards the building of a new church at Red Hill. Not all those present were in favour of the idea, an alternative proposition by Mr C.J.Smith being that the money be used to improve the road from the town to the railway station, and a Mr Thomas Burt proposed that £100 should be allocated to filling in the holes in the roads in the Parish and building a gallery in the existing Reigate church. Both of these suggestions were defeated at the meeting and the money was handed over to the churchwardens.

The following day there was a meeting at Dr Thomas Martin's house in Bell Street, Reigate, to consider what first steps should be taken for erecting a new church at Red Hill. In the chair was the vicar of Reigate, the Rev. R.Snelson, supported by Dr. Martin, William Pearson, William Price, J.Tilley, T.Hart, J.D.Hume and D.Baker. The outcome was a public meeting held at the Town Hall on September 14th, 1840, attended by Earl Somers, his son Lord Eastnor, Lord Jolliffe, and many other prominent figures of the time. Not only was there agreement for the building of the new church but over £1,000 was raised to add to the £411 already in hand. The subscription list eventually topped £3,000, of which £1,000 came from Lord Somers and his son, £600 from the Diocesan Society, and £400 from the Incorporated Society for the

Building of Additional Churches in Populous Parishes. Lady Somers presented a font, Mrs Price the Communion Plate and Mrs Peter Martin and Miss Martin the church bell. Messrs. Nash and Neale, Reigate bankers, were appointed treasurers and Mr Thomas Hart, a solicitor of Church Street, Reigate, the Hon. Secretary. Additionally established was an endowment and repairing fund of £1,500.

On the green to the south of St John's stood Crockerty Well, said to be a recognised meeting place for gossip exchange by local people in the last century. This photograph would appear to show the well, with the church as its backdrop.
(Picture courtesy Freda Welfare)

Three sites for the church were considered. One was on a hill then called Clutton's Site, one on a site called Sawyer's Hill, and the other, the nearest to the present Redhill, on a place referred to as the Knob but also known as Flint's Hill, as it was adjacent to a cottage occupied by a Mr Flint. The one originally chosen was Clutton's Site but a detailed examination of the sub-soil found it unsuitable for burials, and the site finally decided upon was Flint's Hill. Two years later a national school, also partly funded by railway compensation money, was erected on Clutton's Site. All this was common land, and Lord Somers held a Court Baron on September 25th, 1841, and conveyed the land to William Price of Woodhatch, Thomas Neale, the brewer and banker of Reigate, and Robert Clutton of Hartswood, surveyor and land agent, their assigns and heirs for ever.

The design and costs for the church went to public competition and the winner was Mr James Thomas Knowles of Reigate, a man whose family was said to be traceable in that town back to the 16th century. Cost was specified as not to exceed £1,800 and Mr Knowles presented two tenders, one from Robert Hicks of Lambeth at exactly the specified amount, and one from Messrs Comber and Briggs. Mr Comber lived at the top of Whitepost Hill where he had his yard. He ran Redhill 's first post office, although it was only a receiving point and sub-office to Reigate from where deliveries were made. His bid was over the specified amount by £30.15s, but it was his that was accepted. Perhaps it was felt that a local man was to be preferred, and it was difficult to get anyone more local than a mere half mile away. At one of the committee meetings Lord Monson offered to supply white bricks at £4 per 1000 at the kiln, but he was to die in November, 1841, and his works were shut down for a while. Colchester bricks were used and the London and Brighton Railway Company carried them free of charge. The foundation stone was laid by Mrs Cocks on behalf of Earl Somers. The final cost, with the additions of internal decorations, fixtures and fittings, came to £3,800. This included the fir fence with oak posts that was erected around the site and remained until it was replaced with the present wall in 1867. The church was consecrated by the Bishop of Winchester, the area then being in the Winchester Diocese, on September 30th, 1843, and he was assisted by the Vicar of Reigate, the Rev. Filewood Snelson and his churchwardens, George Morrison and Samuel Relf.

The church's architect, Mr Knowles, had designed several large houses in Reigate but was possibly more successful in domestic than ecclesiastical design as the church was not as attractive as it might have been, being functional rather than appealing. It was, however, described in 'The Gentleman's Magazine' for May, 1844, as, '...*an elegant structure with a beautiful spire...calculated to hold 600 persons, two-thirds of the sittings being free...*' That functional design left it bare, cold (only two open fires) and sometimes dark. Services were long and children who attended the day school also had to go to Sunday school in the morning and afternoon, and to church service in-between. Sundays were described as 'sombre and arduous.'

The first incumbent was the Rev. W.Pullen, vicar from 1843-46. He was followed by the Rev. Henry Gosse, 1846-82. The Angel font was installed to commemorate the Rev. Gosse's years. An organ was installed in 1850, and the Father Willis organ installed in 1897.

Around the time the church was built, the Somers Arms coaching Inn at the top of the Brighton Road had lost its custom and subsequently became St. John's parsonage. The Rev. Henry Gosse, vicar for 36 years, continued to live there for many years after resigning the living due to deafness, giving help to the new vicar whenever asked. The new vicar lived at Woodlands House, Woodlands Road, and it may be that the Rev. H.Gosse changed the name of the old parsonage to 'The Firs', if it had not already carried that name. He gave the peal of bells to the church in memory of his wife, Bertha, and erected at his own cost the chancel. He died in 1903.

The Church was originally known as Red Hill District Church and shortly after named St John the Evangelist, although generally known simply as St John's. Its Parish stretched from Gatton to Sidlow, being carved out of St Mary's Parish, and included Little London, Meadvale (then called Mead Hole), Mill Street and Hooley.

Little London grew no more and it was Warwick Town that became the new population centre. Because the St John's area included the new town it remained a Parish with a fast growing population, and the Rev. Gosse, in 1848, had the temporary iron church, St Matthew's Chapel-of-Ease, built in Warwick Town. This was given, it is believed, by Mr Horford, who lived at Batts Hill, and the Rev. Gosse's curate, the Rev. William Kelk, was placed in charge of this booming Parish. The Rev. Kelk, who was described as 'a very good man', was founder of the Mechanics Institute, where the Conservative Club now stands. The Mechanics Institute was, after a time, merged into the YMCA, principally through the efforts of a later St Matthew's curate, the Rev. William Baker. Mr Henry Fowle, the jeweller, was the secretary of the YMCA and also superintendent of St Matthew's Sunday School.

William Kelk died in 1862. When he was replaced in 1862 by the Rev. Henry Brass, St. Matthew's was still part of St John's Parish. The temporary building was rebuilt in 1866 as the present St Matthew's Church and made a separate ecclesiastical Parish in 1867.

At the funeral of the Rev. William Kelk 200 followed the cortege to St John's churchyard and all the shops in the town were closed. In 1867 the flint wall around the church was built in his memory

If the design of St John's church was not too well thought of it seems that its size was also inadequate, for the Reigate, Redhill, Dorking and Epsom Journal of June 18th, 1867, only 24 years after the church was built, gives an account of a public meeting, at which the Bishop of Winchester presided, to consider its enlargement. The church is described as narrow and between high walls, and a design for adding aisles for increased sittings of 536 was submitted by Mr Hesketh (described as an honorary architect). The estimated cost was £3,000 and £1,164 was raised at the meeting. Robert Hesketh's address in the Parliamentary voters list for 1863 was 'near Red Hill church' - he lived at 'The Mount' on Red Hill Common, close to the church and even closer to the third proposed but unused site - and he practised in London. He was born 1817 and died 1880 and sat on the Borough Council from 1870-80.

The aisles were added to the nave of the church in 1869, an addition that did not satisfy requirements for long, for in 1889 the church was largely rebuilt to the design of Mr John Pearson RA, the designer of Truro Cathedral.

The rebuilding took six years, with the new spire being erected in 1895.

There is a story about one of the workmen employed on it losing his nerve and not being able to descend. It is said that his dinner had to be sent up to him, but apparently filling his stomach did not improve his nerve, so he eventually had to be lowered to the ground by rope.

Vicars of St John's	
1843-1846	Rev. W.Pullen
1846-1882	Rev. Henry Gosse
1882-1912	Rev. J.M.Gordon
1912-1924	Rev. B.B.Slater
1924-1926	Rev. C.E.Clarke
1926-1932	Rev. L.G.Mannering
1932-1936	Rev. S.G.Hooper
1936-1937	Rev. Ross MacVicar
1938-1945	Rev. W.A.R.Ball
1945-1955	Rev. J.B.Phillips
1955-1970	Rev. S.C.G.Dyer
1970-1981	Rev. J.Tinsley
1981-1989	Rev. M.J.Goss
1989-1998	Rev. T.Wooderson
1998	Rev. N.Calver

In the 1960s there was concern about movement of the spire when the bells were rung. Not only was there movement but cracks had begun to appear in the structure. In 1972 the bells were lowered by twenty feet to improve weight distribution.

St Joseph's Church

Catholics began to settle in Redhill from the town's earliest inception, which was before the restoration of the Hierarchy of the Catholic Church in this country in 1850. Dr Manning, who was later Cardinal Archbishop of Westminster, said mass at his brother's house at Pendell Court for the first time in 1852, and in subsequent years.

Prior to 1855 Lady Mostyn of Hooley Lodge had converted a room over her stables into a chapel. She eventually bought land next to the Reading Arch where St Joseph's Church, Presbytery and School were built 1860-1. This church was replaced with a new edifice built with £9,000 raised by Father Cavanagh, the rubble of the original church being used for the foundations. The reason for the replacement was that the old church had become both dilapidated and too small. The foundation stone of the new church was laid on August 25th, 1897, and it opened on 27th October, 1898.

There are two accounts of the events surrounding the arrival of the Catholic Sisters in Redhill. The first states that in 1885 four Catholic Sisters and a Mother opened a convent in Cavendish Road and began a day and secondary boarding school for 25 pupils and a primary school for 7 pupils. They moved to Ladbroke Road in 1889 where a chapel and assembly block was opened in 1929, and a new and larger school block in 1937.

The second account says that in 1887 six Sisters of the Christian Retreat took up abode at 'Gore House', near the station. On October 20th, 1890, they moved to Ladbroke Road where they opened a day and boarding school for young ladies and, shortly after, took charge of the Parish School in Chapel

The original St Joseph's Church, partially hidden by the trees, with the Parish School next to it

Road. The Christian Retreat is said to be a London Society established in 1848, of which Redhill was the first branch, although there were others elsewhere afterwards.

Details in these two accounts could easily fit with each other in most respects. More recent history is clearer; the 1937 school block and other

buildings were demolished in the early 1990s and the land given over to housing. St Joseph's Church was demolished in 1986 and rebuilt in a far more modern style on spare ground on the Ladbroke Road site. The modern office block known as Bridge House now occupies the High Street site where the first two St Joseph's Churches once stood.

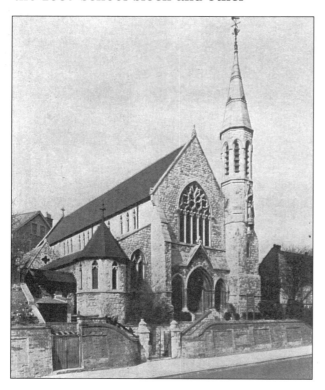

The second St Joseph's Church,
opened 27th October 1897......

...and in the process of
demolition in 1984

Redhill Congregational Church

The original decision to seek to build a Congregational place of worship in Redhill was taken by the Rev. Prout of Reigate in 1858, and in 1859 a site was bought from the S.E.&. C. Railway Co. by benefactor Mr Finch of Tunbridge Wells. Nothing was done immediately, but in January, 1861, the Rev. Prout convened a meeting at Hooley Cottage, Redhill, the home of Mr Richardson, of interested persons and the decision to proceed

with the project was taken. The committee formed included Mr Richardson himself, Mr Williamson of London Road, Mr Bennett of Linkfield Lane, and Mr Henry Fowle.

Early Congregational services were held at the Market Hall from March, 1861, while work progressed. One account states that the Congregational Church in Chapel Road opened in January, 1862, another that the foundation stone was laid in February of that year and the opening date was in September. This latter would seem to be correct, as the first service was held on October 2nd, 1862. The overall cost of the accommodation for 600 seats - 100 in a gallery - was £2,500. The large school hall was built shortly after.

The Rev. W.P.Dothie was the first minister, staying for 14 years. He was followed in 1876 by the Rev. Herbert Stent, who was succeeded in 1882 by the Rev. James McKenzie. He left in 1891 and the Rev. John Gardner took over in the following year. The Rev. Andrew Leggatt followed him in 1905.

The Rev. Leggatt benefited from the generosity of Miss Whitley of Upper Bridge Road, who at her own expense had a manse built for the incumbent of the Congregational Church. Built in Ridgeway Road on part of the Garlands estate the house enjoys the view across the valley to Redstone Hill.

The building was designed by Messrs

The rear elevation of the Ridgeway Road manse (Picture Courtesy Surrey Mirror)

Hooper and Son, and a commemorative plaque by the front door was designed by Vincent Hooper. The house, now in private ownership, may have also served as a design 'sampler' for prospective customers of the architect to view, as it is of a multitude of styles, having one wall tile hung, one rendered, one brown brick and one red brick. There are also various types and styles of windows and other features incorporated within it.

The turn of the century saw the building of the Presbyterian Church of St Paul's at Shaws Corner, and dissension drew to it worshippers from the Congregational Church. In 1972 the Congregational and Presbyterian Churches became united and reformed and St Paul's became the Redhill United Reformed Church.

The Chapel Road Congregational Church continued, its large hall at one time being home to the Redhill library. Problems with the hall led to the vacation of the entire premises in 1988, the demolition of the hall in 1991, and the subsequent demolition of the church in 1993, as no buyer for it could be found. During the demolition a poster for a 'Sacred Concert', held on October 8th, 1890, was found. The poster had

Miss Sarah Whitley, who presented the manse to the Redhill Congregational Church, and was herself presented with a silver key to the house by the church (Picture courtesy Surrey Mirror)

been hidden between blocked-off walls for over one hundred years.

The site is now occupied by modern flats, only the stone front wall remaining. The congregation transferred to St Paul's.

The Congregational Church and Hall

St Matthew's Church

The first services in what was to become St Matthew's Parish were held in Lonsdale House, Warwick Road, which was the first church and the first school. A brick and wood building with a slated roof (other accounts say it was an iron building) was then built in about 1855-7 on the site of the present church and was the temporary church for 10-11 years. The Rev. Kelk was the first minister and is referred to in the part of this chapter dealing with St. John's. He was succeeded by the Rev. Brass in 1863.

A brick infants school was built close by on part of the site, the whole having previously been allotments, and was bounded by a hedge. It was in the St

Matthew's infants school where the historic first meeting was held that began the movement for incorporation and the Council we have today.

The decision to build a new church was taken in 1863 and a letter was sent to Lord Monson asking him to sell the freehold of the land. A preliminary and influential meeting was held in December, 1863, in the infants school room, to discuss the reply, in which Lord Monson consented, and a motion was unanimously carried to the effect that Mr Webb be instructed to effect the purchase. In the event no purchase was necessary, for not only did Lord Monson give the ground but he also gave money towards the new construction.

There was a public meeting at the Redhill Market Hall to promote the new church for the district of Warwick Town, at which the Bishop of Winchester presided, and there were also present on the platform Lord Monson, Archdeacon

St Matthews' Church

Mitterton, the Rev J.Fry (hon. sec), the Reverends J.N.Harrison, A Cazenove, H.Brass, H.Gosse, J.C.Wynter (rural dean), Mr Gooch (Master of the Grammar School), J.Hawke, G.C.Richardson Esq. and others.

The foundation stone of St Matthew's Church, Warwick Town, was laid on a Tuesday afternoon in March, 1865, by the Rt Hon. Lord Monson. The building was designed in the early-decorated style and built of Reigate Stone with Bath Stone dressings. The architect was Mr J.M.K.Hahn of Kings Road, Bedford Road, London, and Mr Carruthers of Reigate was the builder. The cost was not to exceed £5,000 and it was intended eventually to build a parsonage house. The Bishop of Winchester was again present to consecrate the new building in June, 1866.

The Rev. Henry Brass in 1878
(Courtesy Holmesdale Natural History Club)

The Rev. Brass and child
(Courtesy Holmesdale Natural History Club)

Early depiction of St Matthew's Church on a souvenir cup

1932 sketch of the proposed new Central Hall and buildings (Courtesy Surrey Mirror)

Methodist Church, Brighton Road: Central Hall, London Road

The foundation stone of the Brighton Road Methodist Church was laid in 1884. Due to lack of seating and road problems a move to another site in Brighton Road was considered for many years before the Methodist Central Hall in London Road was built. The new facility opened in April, 1934, on a site once home to the old Redhill Bowling Club, part of the green remaining until the 1990s. White inside, the main hall had tip-up seats, a novelty at the time, seating 500 on the ground floor and 230 in the balcony. It had a billiard room, a Sunday school and a film screen. On opening day Sir Joseph Rank was in the choir and six policemen were needed to regulate the crowd.

The Brighton Road church eventually closed and was put up for sale in 1954. It was used as business premises before final redevelopment. In 1958 the Central Hall was being established as a centre for Methodist worship, possibly at the expense of groups such as the local Choral Society who had given performances there since 1941. The whole site was redeveloped in the 1990s with the Methodist Hall being rebuilt with improved facilities for worship as well as general use.

The Brighton Road Methodist Chapel can be seen on the left foreground in this picture of the 'Old Crocks' run from the 1960s or 70s

The 1934 Central Hall in process of demolition in the 1990s

An unusual view of the new Methodist Hall, made possible by the demolition of the telephone exchange next door

The Philanthropic Farm School Chapel

For the boys who lived and worked at the Farm School this might have been a warmer place to be on winter Sunday mornings than some of the alternatives on offer. Built in 1848/9, today only its front porch survives. Pictures of the church appear in chapter 4.

Primitive Methodist Chapel, Meadvale

The Primitive Methodists are said to have been the first non-conformists to hold services in Redhill, hiring in 1854 the school of Mr Holden, which stood where the Conservative Club now stands. They did not stay there long but built their chapel in Lower Road, Meadvale in 1855.

St Anne's Chapel

This chapel had its foundation stone laid by the Prince and Princess of Wales in 1884 and served first the St Anne's Society and later the Foundling School, which both occupied the large redbrick building that for many years dominated the site. The story of St Anne's is to appear in volume 2 of this history.

The chapel was the subject of some controversy in the 1970s when it was found that its stained glass windows had been sold to an American buyer and lost to the Borough and the Country.

Redhill Presbyterian Church of St Paul's, now Redhill United Reformed Church

Two of the founders of this church were Howard Waters and John Hill Duncan. Mr Duncan was born in Peebles in 1848 and was a grandson of Dr Henry Duncan, founder of the Savings Bank. He came to Redhill in 1893 and lived at a house called Hollycroft, close to the joining of Redstone Hill and Nutfield Road, Redhill. He became a president of the YMCA and a governor of the Colman Institute. Presbyterian worship began at the Market Hall and continued there for six weeks of 1900 until a temporary building was ready at Shaws Corner. The site had been bought from Mr R.S.Nicol, who accepted the same price as had been asked of Reigate Corporation when they were looking for a site for the Municipal Buildings (a subject that will be dealt with in vol.2 of this history). Mr Waters had been the Corporation negotiator and, because the site was not taken by the Corporation, negotiated the sale for the church instead. The permanent church was built at a cost of £7,500 and opened on the 28th May, 1902. This was at a time when dissension brought to it many of the worshippers from the Congregational Church in Chapel Road.

A temporary minister, the Rev. James Rennie, came from Scotland and stayed nine months. The first permanent minister was the Rev. J.M.E.Ross. The first elders were Mr J.Hill Duncan, Mr W.Figg, Mr Stanley Gray and Mr W.Walker. Mr C.D.Morton, who had been the chairman of the building committee, was the first treasurer. Mr J.Hill Duncan died in January, 1911.

In 1972 the Congregational and Presbyterian Churches became united and reformed and St Paul's became Redhill United Reformed Church.

Holy Trinity Church

Standing at the corner of the Brighton and Carlton Roads, this church was built to serve a Parish formed from the northern part of St Matthew's. The proposal to build the church was made in 1905 and services were held in a temporary Holy Trinity Church at St Matthew's Mission Rooms until the new building was ready. The foundation stone was laid by Lord Ashcombe in May, 1906, and the new church was dedicated to the Rev. Brass, who was for over 40 years vicar of St Matthew's. Consecration took place in January, 1907, and the Rev. L.A.McClintoch Newbery was inducted as first vicar that May. Total cost of the new building was around £10,000, the site costing £590 and the building itself £8,000.

The Baptist Chapel, Station Road

The room in Holden's Rooms used by the Primitive Methodists was also used by the Strict (or Particular) Baptists who, in 1845, had met at a warehouse at the Redhill Tannery owned by Ebenezer Hooper. The Baptist Chapel, once standing alone but today squashed between neighbouring buildings in Station Road, Redhill, bears the date of 1858 proudly on its front, and Ebenezer Hooper was closely involved in its development. A very early picture of the chapel appears on page 68.

The Wesleyan Chapel, The Wesleyan Church

The Wesleyans built a house (late 1850s-early 1860s) whose ground floor was a large room where services were held. It was later occupied by Mr Berrett, draper, but it is uncertain whether the building referred to was his shop in High Street or his house, Holmewood Villa, at the corner of Grovehill and Upper Bridge Roads (probably the former). The Wesleyan Chapel in Woodlands Road was erected in 1878 and the church in Station Road West in 1882, the latter, a large and fairly ornate edifice, was demolished in the 1960s.

The New Primitive Methodist Chapel

This was built in Brighton Road by Mr J.Hall of Sutton for £303. The foundation stone was laid in August, 1870, by Councillor F.J.Besley to whom the Rev W.Dinnick presented a history of the Primitive Methodist Society, saying it would show that the Primitive Methodists were, 'the most wonderful people on the face of the earth.' The architect was R.Collet Esq.

Christian Scientists Hall, London Road

This hall stood between The Gatton Point public house and the adjacent maisonettes. It began life as a large conservatory attached to a large house called The Lodge, the grounds of which included the site of the petrol station at Gatton Point. The building was converted to a games room, then to a small bungalow, and then was used as a meeting place for the Christian Scientists. It was afterwards used as business premises before being demolished at the same time as The Gatton Point public house in 1998.

The Baptist Chapel

The Baptists began their activities in the Market Hall before settling, in 1866, in their chapel in London Road, Redhill, a site that in 1999 is the site of Boots' opticians, Tru-Fi etc. The situation was a perfectly good one in 1866 but the road that once passed its door became too busy and the congregation sold up and built a new Baptist Church at Hatchlands Road in 1959.

The small parade of shops that replaced the chapel were set back as though a new building line was to be established on the west side of the London Road, but little other rebuilding was undertaken and today the shops still sit back as though separated from their neighbours.

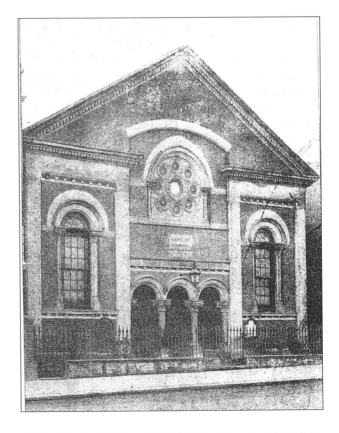

The Baptist Chapel, Brighton Road, now the site of shops.

PICKFORDS
FOR REMOVALS and WAREHOUSING.
EXPERIENCED PACKERS.

ESTIMATES AND ADVICE FREE.

MODERATE CHARGES.

Rail and Steamship
Tickets Issued.

Berths Booked by All
Principal Lines.

SETTLER'S EFFECTS
PACKED and SHIPPED.

93 Brighton Rd., REDHILL.

'Phone. No 225.

Continued Growth and Development

1860 - 1879

Although the creation of the Borough of Reigate by grant of Charter of Incorporation by Queen Victoria in 1863 ranks as the major event of the time, there were plenty of other things happening in and around Redhill to interest those of us who now look back at the years up to the end of the century. Some were events examined elsewhere in this history, but whether major or minor, those included here give a flavour of life in the years up to 1900.

In these early days there must have been a pioneer atmosphere that propelled Redhill towards an era of boom and prosperity. If you were at the leading edge of the thrust towards continuing development then there was good money to be made, but if you were in the less prosperous trailing caravan then life had its ups and downs. The truth probably was that the majority was dependent upon the minority to provide work and wages so were not masters of their own destinies. They raised their families as best they could in cramped and overcrowded accommodation, working long hours in poor conditions and seeing no security in approaching old age.

A good example of the contrast between the classes was provided on the east side of town where, in 1860, James Ladbroke built Ladbroke Road from his estate at Frenches for personal access to the railway station, while the Redhill and Reigate Cottage Improvement Society, formed to provide working class properties, of which there was a shortage, built thirty-one cottages between that road and the railway.

Station Road West, with residences at one end and businesses at the other, connected the brand new town centre, the focus of much activity, with Linkfield Corner, a road junction connecting the old to the new. This junction was itself transformed by a railway line to Reigate that created sounds and sights not seen there before, to which were added smells from the tannery when the wind was in the right direction. The Globe Temperance Hotel was built there in 1861, and Bashford's furniture store was to occupy a commanding position nearby.

Closer to the new town more businesses sprang up. A.J.Dulake, tea and grocery merchant (*Reading biscuits fresh once a week*) was in situ by 1861, as was William Best's butcher's shop (*Families supplied on the most favourable terms*). At 24 Station Road West, on the corner of Warwick Terrace, was.......

MARY WILLETT
Fancy bread and Biscuit Baker
**PASTRYCOOK &
CONFECTIONER**
Corn Dealer &c
STATION ROAD AND NEAR THE
CHURCH, REDHILL
*Families supplied with genuine
Home-made, brown and Welsh
Breads*

.......and next door to her, at 26, was Thomas Lanaway, ironmonger and maker of stoves and ranges.

Miss Morgan, bookseller, Frederick

Bonny, Tailor, Hatter and Hosier, and F.Wallis, plumber, painter and glazier were not far away. Arthur Wood, successor to J.Brinsmead and Sons, had set up his music business in the road and Henry Summers carried on a ladies' fashion shop at Commerce House, possibly starting there when the premises were built in the early 1860s. He became a councillor and was Mayor from 1886-8.

Parts of the town that had not existed a few years before were throwing up businesses and it was in the early sixties when buildings were put up on the east side of the High Street, south of the Market Field. The 1861 census provides the basic facts that reveal the local rate of growth. In 1861 there were 1,583 inhabited dwellings in Reigate Town and Foreign combined. By 1871 there were 2,584 houses, and by 1881 the 1861 figure had more than doubled to 3,192, compared to a mere 417 in 1801. The emergent and spreading new development had turned the vicinity from a rural backwater into a rapidly expanding residential and business area.

One single thing that could perhaps be identified with these times was the horse. Horses gave people their main motive force on the roads and in the fields until other forms of power such as steam, petrol and diesel engines provided the means of moving people and goods. Such was the horse's presence that many facets of present times still remind us of its past importance. A few domestic buildings still have the archways that provided access to courtyards and stables at the rear. Some business premises still retain their arched entrances under which horses pulled carts laden with raw materials inwards and products outwards, or coaches in the case of inns and hotels. Some have loft doors over their front entrance through which loads were hauled when arched ways to the rear were not available. Marriage's shop

in Redhill had this feature at its rear. Iron tethering rings still hang on some house walls, and we are all familiar with the horse troughs, nowadays filled with flowers instead of water, which still stand beside roads used as main supply routes.

A feature connected directly with the horse, and just as rarely seen now, is the smithy. Those still working earlier this century were places of great attraction to children, with the roar of the fire, the sound of the bellows, the hiss of the hot shoe dropped into water to cool, the patient horse looking over its shoulder as it was shod; all this and more was the smithy.

It is easy to romanticise about such places, however. Probably the children were chased off by a smith who worked hard and long hours for small wages. Blacksmiths did not just shoe horses but took on other work, such as repairing farm implements, fences, carriages and carts, and as motorcars became popular they took to repairing them as well. Eventually blacksmiths were doing more work on cars than on horses, and many smithies turned into the forerunners of the garages we have today.

In April, 1861, when the meeting rooms and corn exchange at the Market Hall were providing a brand new facility in Redhill, the building of a Public Hall in Reigate High Street was begun, creating a similar facility there. With building work finishing at the end of the year, Peter Martin, son of the then still Bailiff of the Manor of Reigate, Thomas Martin, presided over the dinner held on the 15th January, 1862, in celebration of the opening of the new hall. In the same month there was an advertisement in a local paper for the post office in the premises of F. Allwork, dispensary and family chemist of Station Road, Redhill, with the added information that the chemist side of the business had been established in 1849. For around ten years the Redhill post office remained in a back room of the chemist shop, with Mr Allwork as Postmaster, and three postmen delivering to Redhill, Chipstead, Meadvale, Earlswood and Merstham. His retirement in 1866 was followed by Mr Cole being appointed Postmaster.

Mr E.H.Cole, Red Hill Postmaster, 1866 (Courtesy Reigate and Banstead Council)

It was in 1862 that the Caterham Spring Water Company came into being and was eventually to be the provider of mains water to Redhill. Water was especially necessary for spraying onto the unmetalled roads to prevent their break-up during droughts. The surfacing of roads as we know it today was still fifty years in the future. An item in an1863 newspaper article following some hot summer weather noted, *'The past week has reminded us that the time has come round again when the roads might need to be watered. Some steps are being taken that it shall be done this season.'*

St Mark's Church, Reigate, was opened just prior to Incorporation and, in November came the death of Mr Peter Martin, who had recently presided at the opening of Reigate Public Hall. Two Redhill traders of the time were Mr E.S.Lambert, running a tailoring business, established in 1857, at 5 Station Road, and Mr J.Symonds of Hatchlands Farm, who was advertising...

> POTATOES POTATOES!!
> Good store potatoes delivered at the following prices:-
> Flukes 7s per sack, Scotch Red 6s .

The collection of road tolls at this time was put into the hands of private enterprise via the announcement: -

FOXLEY HATCH GATE, HOOLEY LANE GATE, MERSTHAM GATE, RAY COMMON GATE and GATTON TOLL BAR will be let by auction to the best bidder at the Grey-hound Inn, Croydon, on Saturday the 10th day of October next at one o'clock p.m. precisely, for 12 calendar months from 12 o'clock at noon of the 1st day of January 1864. These Tolls were let by auction for the present year at the net sum of £800, clear of salaries, for collecting same..... ...Dated 7th day of September 1863. Wm. Drummond, Clerk to the Trustees.

The Surrey Gazette of November 6th, 1863, reported that the wind had been blowing a stiff south westerly for several weeks and eventually, *'blew a perfect hurricane'* to cause considerable damage in the neighbourhood. A villa that was being erected on Furze Hill, and was roofed and slated, fell prey to its fury. The villa, said to be a first-class building consisting of three floors and about 24 rooms, was valued between £800 and £900 when finished, and as it was around half finished at the time of the gale the damage was placed at about £300 or £400. The entire loss fell on the builder, Mr Gage, of West Street, Warwick Town (name still in use in 1863), the villa with two others being built on speculation. No one was injured, the men having left work a short time before. A part of the building was blown down at a quarter to six in the evening, another part on Saturday morning, which left only the back wall of the villa standing. This swayed back and forth with the wind so some men set to work with poles and pushed it down to prevent injury to anyone. All of this was no doubt an event that lived on in the memory of Mr Gage. (West Street was later renamed Cromwell Road)

Also in November of 1863 a new Lodge of Odd Fellows, the Prince of Wales Lodge, was opened at the Tower Inn, High Street, Redhill. Thirteen persons enrolled their names as members. Supper was provided at eight o'clock by the worthy host Mr Topliss, to which about 40 sat down.

At the end of the month a vestry meeting was held in the hall of the Corn Exchange for the purpose of electing two inspectors for the lighting board of Linkfield borough in place of two retiring members. Incorporation might now be

upon Redhill but some Borough business had to continue as in manorial days until the new Corporation could get around to assuming such duties.

It was the following year when the Borough police force was formed and the Fullers Earth pits were sold by auction by the executors of the late owner. If there was a sign that Redhill was up-and-coming in no uncertain fashion surely nothing signified the fact more than a notice in the Surrey Standard of February 20th, 1864:

London and County Bank
Redhill Branch

With a view to meeting the convenience of the inhabitants of Redhill and the growing importance of the place, this branch will, on and after Tues 16th inst., be open daily instead of once a week as heretofore

Isaac Marsh, Manager. Feb 13th 1864

High Street, Redhill, in the last century, looking towards the Reading Arch. The unmetalled state of the road can easily be seen. The tall building on the right stands on the site of the present day Woolworth's.

This was the year when work on the first London Underground route began and, in Redhill, the name of Workhouse Lane was changed to Hatchlands Road.

At a time when a meeting at the Tower Inn decided to form a Redhill fire brigade (more about this in chapter 14) William Berrett began trading in the High Street. By now the Brighton Road also had businesses serving the community on the south side of town, and more were coming. The Anchor public house was built on the corner of Grovehill and Brighton Roads, and John Stoneman came from Devon to establish his funeral business in premises a little further along the Brighton Road, remaining there for eleven years before moving to Cromwell Road in 1876.

A vestry meeting was held at the Market Hall in March, 1864, to discuss widening the road at Shaws Corner. It was considered to be dangerous and a proposal to increase the width from 16 to 30 feet as far as Reffells Bridge was unanimously agreed. Mr J.Symon's tender for £340 was accepted, the next nearest bid being £394. This was again the kind of matter still being dealt with by petty boroughs, in this case Linkfield, but the new Council was busy establishing itself and getting around to dealing with all local affairs.

In January, 1866, heavy snow followed by a rapid thaw flooded lower town areas, with the east end of Station Road submerged. Stoneman's Cottages in Ladbroke Road were over a foot deep in water and the inhabitants had to get in and out by means of ladders to the upper windows. Cellars of the Wheatsheaf and South Eastern Hotels were flooded. In February an unusually severe storm again flooded all lower portions of the town, many people suffering further considerable damage to their property.

In April, 1867, a report of the Highways and Works Committee recommended that the road from the top of Redstone Hill to the Somers Arms Inn at Linkfield Corner should be adopted by the Corporation. Stringent conditions attached included getting money from the Railway Company to put the road in repair, plus indemnification against having to widen the railway arch, which meant that the road's adoption was to be delayed for some considerable time.

This year also marked the passing of an era, with the death in August of Thomas Martin of Reigate, the manorial Bailiff who had convened the very first meeting for incorporation.

A Sewerage Works and a Pleasure Ground

In 1867 the Corporation applied for permission to borrow £4,000 to buy 16 acres of the top of Red Hill Common as a means whereby 50 to 70 more acres elsewhere could be obtained for a sewerage works.

This might sounds a rather strange way of doing things but what had happened was that the best site for the outfall for the drainage system the Corporation was building had been identified as land at the bottom of Earlswood Common, and the Council had accordingly applied to Earl Somers to grant it to them.

In 1862 the Secretary for War had compulsorily purchased 16 acres on the summit of Red Hill Common for a military prison. About one third of the purchase money, some £1,000, had been paid to Lord Somers, and two thirds to five trustees for the persons entitled to common rights. Owing to the number and intricacy of the common rights titles, the trustees had considered the distribution of the funds in their hands to be impracticable, so none had so far been attempted.

The War office had since given up the idea of erecting a military prison on the land and the Corporation had opened negotiations with a view to acquiring it as a public pleasure ground, making

Redhill Common.

A brick pillar stands out on the skyline on Red Hill Common. It was used as a sighting point during the 1842 building of the long, straight stretch of the Dover railway line beyond the Philanthropic School. After completion the pillar remained with a seat around it, but in the 1930s it was converted into a memorial for the 25th Jubilee of King George V.

simultaneous overtures to two parties - the Secretary of War for the purchase of the land and the trustees of the Commoners, with the aim of obtaining from them the £2,000 and using it as part payment of the purchase cost, but after protracted negotiations attempts to retrieve the money from the trustees failed through the unshakeable objection of one of these men to hand it over.

Lord Somers proposed that on the condition that the trustees' £2,000 was disregarded, and that the Corporation purchased out of its own resources the piece of land on the summit of Red Hill for a public pleasure ground, and also that the Mayor, aldermen and burgesses entered into proper deed of covenant with the Lord, his heirs and assigns, for the perpetual use and enjoyment of the land by the inhabitants of the Borough, his Lordship would grant the land at Earlswood Common.

The legal wheels were put in motion. Conveyance of all land was approved and the Corporation borrowed £4,000 against the rates to defray the cost, £1,000 of which was for fencing, ditching, levelling and laying out the land. It was an unusual arrangement but the merits of it were that the Corporation became the proprietors of two sites, each suited for the purpose for which it was acquired, and at an overall cost of about £40 an acre, the current price in the area then being from £200 to £300 an acre. It was a deal that benefits us all to the present day.

The aims of the United Land Company were the purchase of freehold and leasehold property of every description, the purchase of estates, and the subdivision of estates into parts. The purpose was development and an area so developed in 1868 was the Waterslade Estate. Bounded by Hatchlands Road and Red Hill Common, three new roads were cut through it for building frontages and were called Ranelagh, Shrewsbury and Brownlow Roads. Viscount Ranelagh and Col. Brownlow

Knox MP were chairman and vice chairman respectively of the company. There were upwards of eighty other peers and notable persons associated as directors and shareholders, and Shrewsbury was the name of one of the more prominent of these.

The name Waterslade is basically a reference to meadowland with water, the water coming from the springs that occur in the area around Whitepost Hill. Perhaps this spring, and the area it watered and where animals once drank created the pond referred to in 1882 by a newspaper article which reported, *'Our suggestion as to the clearing out of the pond at the Cottage Hospital has been carried out and a great improvement is the result....we hope the pond may be kept clean.....by making an example of one of the little ragamuffins who amuse themselves by filling it full of rubbish.'*

Warwick Brewery, in Warwick Town, was put up for sale in August, 1869, on

The name of the Waterslade Spring was engraved on the white block on the brick cowl built over it.

instructions of representatives of the late Mr Stephen Clifton. It included, *'a comfortable house with excellent cellars and storage possessing considerable frontage to the Station Road and complete brewery premises in rear, comprising brick built brew house, malt store, vat store, four stalled stable.....good yard. Premises at present in occupation of Mr W.A.Towns, brewer, who carries on an important trade.'*

In the same month the progress of the sewerage work was being reported to the Council by the Town Clerk, who read a report from Mr B.Latham, the designer of the Redhill drainage system, on progress of the irrigation works on the land obtained from Lord Somers. Also presented was a plan for a main sewer from Reigate Town to Earlswood Common, including piping of sewage from the then outfall in Park Lane, on the Priory pond, to the same irrigation works on Earlswood Common via a route under Park Hill.

In November the Town Clerk finally presented the conveyance of Station Road to the Council and it was ordered to be signed. It had been four years since the first recommendation that the road be adopted by the Corporation.

The 1870s

Sydney Jennings came to Redhill in 1870 and worked for some years for a Redhill family of tea merchants named Ashby. He subsequently went into a cycle business on the west side of London Road, a few shops north of the Queens Arms public house, with a partner named Keen, possibly before setting up at 13, High Street.

Number 13 became 27 when the High Street was renumbered, probably to take account of development on both sides of the road, and at that address in the 1880s both Jennings and Keen were trading. The tea business was not given up, for at number 12, High Street, was

Jennings' shop at 27 High Street towards the end of the 19th century.

S.C. Jennings' tea warehouse. Jennings' shop at 27 was to last several generations and see more than one site but fell foul of development and changing market patterns in the 1990s.

The Redhill post office was becoming more and more extensive. It had entered the era of electrical technology by acquiring the electric telegraph, which was run on its behalf by the Electric Telegraph Company. In 1870 the Government acquired the Telegraphs and the operators became P.O. employees.

In 1872 came the opening of the new St Matthew's Boys School by the Bishop of Winchester. The state of local schools had been recently criticised and the possibility of establishing a School

Board had loomed. The general feeling was said to be that a School Board, which was the face of the state regulation of education, would add to the rate burden, but this may have been a good way of creating opposition to a scheme in which the churches thought that their brand of religious education might suffer. A newspaper report stated, *'The general desire to further the cause of education, and a specific desire to avoid the establishment of a School Board, with its possible tending to secular education, have led to the erection of a new National School for Boys for the district of St Matthew's, Red Hill, just as the same causes led but recently to the establishment of a new Wesleyan day school in the same district. The new building has been erected by Mr Curruthers under contract from designs gratuitously furnished by Mr Hesketh of the Mount, Red Hill. - Lite (sic) behind Girls school presented by Rev. H.Brass.'*

The Borough population was past the 16,000 mark when in 1872 the death occurred at Hooley Lodge of Constantia, Lady Mostyn, the most stalwart of the keepers of the Roman Catholic faith in Redhill. She passed away on 12th December aged 65, and was buried in Reigate cemetery.

In Clair Grece's grandmother's diary of 23rd January, 1875, is written, *'Dr Grece with Mr William Stenning to see a gentleman at Worsted Green about a projected new road from the station to Godstone.'* The road was the A25 and Dr Grece was of the opinion that instead of continuing up the steep Redstone Hill it needed to be turned east where Cavendish Road is and continued to Nutfield Marsh, or better still continued to join the road to Oxted at Tylers Green, Godstone. This would at one stroke have doubled the value of all the land along the route and substitute a hill-less road for the present camel back road to Nutfield and Bletchingley. As we know

The cattle market, Redhill, a regular addition to the commercial activity of the town.

this was never done, but it is interesting to consider the changes such a project would have brought about.

Robert Phillips came to Redhill around 1880 and started Phillips' Stores in the Brighton Road, immediately next to the Reading Arch, in 1881. He remained there for many years, and some of the adverts whitewashed onto the walls of the building are still readable in the late 1990s.

Lawn Tennis

In 1879 a group of people leased a plot of land between linkfield Lane and Carlton Road from lord monson and formed the Redhill Croquert and Lawn Tennis Club. Croquet was given up after the !st World War but tennis is still played on the same site.

ROYAL OAK HOTEL,

HIGH STREET, REDHILL.

Proprietress - Mrs. CHALWIN.

SALOON BAR.

Nalder & Collyer's Indian Pale Ale.

EXCELLENT WINES AND SPIRITS.

Redhill Tradesmen's Slate Club.

Two Local Services
The Stories of the Borough Police and Fire Brigade

The Police Force

The first 'police' in Reigate manorial days were borough and parish constables and it was not until 1851 when a police presence other than these was established by Surrey in London Road, Redhill. It later moved to Reigate and at one time there was a sergeant and six constables for whom the parish paid into the County rate.

Incorporation in 1863 was followed by the creation of the Borough of Reigate's own force in 1864. There was to be a Superintendent at £90 p.a. plus quarters, a sergeant at 21/- p.w. and 8 constables at 18/- p.w. The first Head Constable was George Gifford but he lasted only nine days and was succeeded by George Rogers who held the post for many years. The station house was at 3, Carlton Terrace, Redhill, alongside the Market Hall, but as there were no lock-up facilities prisoners had to be catered for elsewhere until a house in West Street, Reigate, was rented at £25 p.a. and the cellar was converted to two cells.

In August of 1864 consideration was given to the siting of a central police station near Shaws Corner and land for the purpose was purchased from Mr Waterlow. The project never got under way and the land deal was eventually reversed. A new police station was built alongside the Market Hall in 1866 and became the headquarters for the two towns. Reigate's station remained, although it was moved from West Street to premises between the Public Hall and the Congregational Church. The title of Superintendent of Police was changed to Head Constable in 1870.

In these early years, hours and conditions were onerous, as were the rules - *'No PC to leave the borough without permission, nor to be in the borough out of uniform whether on or off duty'* - and the behaviour of the locals left something to be desired, for in May of 1882 the Watch Committee resolved, *'That the Head Constable take steps to render the High Street more orderly on a Saturday evening.'* Perhaps Saturday nights in Red Hill had always been rowdy, for the Watch Committee minutes of November, 1864, authorised the Superintendent to, *'buy new hat to replace one destroyed by crowd.'*

George Rogers, Borough Police Superintendent 1864-88.
(Courtesy Reigate and Banstead Council)

It is often said that 'you just can't get the staff', with the meaning that those you do get are less than satisfactory. This seems to have fitted the case of the early police force: -

1864   PC Stovell fined 2/6d for misconduct
1864   PC Dashwood discharged
1864   PC Foss reprimanded
1864   PC Stovell discharged
1864   PC Ison told to be more respectful
1864   PC Harling convicted for stealing
1864   PC Foss reprimanded - fined 5/-
1864   PC Serjeant reprimanded for exposing an immoral article
1864   PC Naughton reprimanded - fined 1 day's pay
1864   PC Stuart reprimanded and fined
1864   PC Ison reprimanded and fined 1 day's pay

1865   PC Baugh reprimanded and dismissed for being drunk
1865   PC Taylor dismissed
1866   PC Beddington dismissed for being drunk
1866   PC Moss dismissed for being absent
1871   PC Lewis dismissed for drinking with poachers
1874   PC Whiteland dismissed for being found in a house of ill fame
1894   Head Constable Philip Woodman imprisoned for embezzlement

The Borough of Reigate Police Force in 1879 outside the Redhill Police Station in Carlton Place, which was alongside the Market Hall, Redhill. Head Constable George Rogers is on the left.
(Picture courtesy Holmesdale Natural History Club)

George Rogers was followed in 1888 by William Pearson, who resigned in 1891 and was replaced by William Morant. In 1894 Philip Woodman was appointed but was fairly soon arrested for embezzling police funds at his previous employment in the Bradford police force. Then came James Metcalfe, who ended this period of change at the top by remaining for 36 years.

At the turn of the century there were two inspectors, four sergeants and twenty-eight constables. The 1901/2 Municipal Buildings at Reigate made provision for a brand new police headquarters station and cells in the basement with stairs leading to the court, now the council chamber, on the first floor. The Head Constable moved into his new house alongside and the Reigate station was sold.

The Redhill station had become far too small for the increased size of the force and extra responsibilities, such as weights and measures. It was no longer the force HQ but remained as the local station. Accommodation at the new Reigate building was also to become too small, however, as the size of both force and Council increased steadily. The result was that the Reigate police presence was moved to a house called Cherchefelle, in Chart Lane.

The following year William Beacher succeeded James Metcalfe and adopted the title of Chief Constable rather than Head Constable. Having seen military service as well as previous police service the new man was an accomplished horseman and was often to be seen on duty in the area on horseback, although he also had an official car.

Athletics was also an interest of his, and not just as a spectator, as he was winner of a 100 yards handicap race at one of the police sports events.

Few early postcards of the centre of Redhill fail to show a policeman on point duty. It must have been quite a

The original motorcycle cops in the Borough, Jock Mason and R.Brownlow, were first seen patrolling the streets in 1931/2. Here PC Mason is seen on his machine in 1932.

contrast for local residents when this familiar figure was replaced by traffic lights in the early 1930s. This innovation was something that had been pressed for by the Home Office for a considerable time, the main gain being the manpower saving. More of this was achieved around the same period when it became a fire brigade task to drive the ambulance, although control of the vehicle remained with the police.

At Redhill, in 1932, purpose-built premises were opened in London Road for the combined presence of police and fire brigade. Closer co-operation this year between police and fire brigade at Reigate took the form of one of the firemen being paid to take care of stray dogs kept at the police station there.

The Special Constabulary was in existence at this time and one of the re-organisations undertaken by Mr Beacher was the formation of a Special Constabulary Mobile Section - a kind of 'Flying Squad' - under Special Chief Inspector Sir Malcolm Campbell. With such a man in charge it is not surprising that the two sections formed comprised one of 'moderately fast cars' and another of 'super fast cars'.

While on the subject of the 'Flying Squad', another innovation organised by the Chief Constable in 1935 was that of a local aviation branch at Redhill Aerodrome, the first of its kind in the country. Twelve machines and pilots were on call for aerial search purposes with police on board as observers.

Chief Constable Beacher remained in the post until the Borough force was merged into a new Surrey force during WW2 when he became Superintendent of the Reigate Division. The station at Cherchefelle closed in 1972 when the new Reigate Road Station opened. The Redhill station closed soon after and the centralisation of the force in the two towns, first envisaged 108 years before, was effectively complete.

Inspector James King, who retired in 1899 after almost 32 years service in the Borough of Reigate police force

The advance of technology has greatly influenced modern police methods. Here the Mayor of Reigate, Councillor Horsfall, is shown the CCTV facilities at Reigate Police Station in 1995.

The men of the 1919 Reigate Police Force outside the Reigate Municipal Buildings.

More About George Rogers

In his 1901 book, '*Reigate, Home and Foreign, Past and Present*', E.Harcourt Burrage writes about Head Constable Rogers, portraying him as the last of a class of official who had a knack of making things comfortable for both the local inhabitants and himself in a way that was to be admired. E.Harcourt Burrage lived at Earlswood but probably never knew the Head Constable personally. He was a Borough Councillor for a number of years so would have had ample opportunity to learn about the doings of the man from others who had known him.

He describes George Rogers as a man of diplomatic complaisance and calm endurance, one who was no oppressor of the weak and sinful but liked to think of himself as an official whose hand of iron was gloved in

velvet, and whose qualities were appreciated. A man of portly form through many years of substantial living he liked such appreciation be expressed in things nourishing, but the writer stresses that no man should insinuate that Mr Rogers was ever bribed, saying that he was not a man to betray his office for lucre. He just had a desire to make his official presence and duties as little irksome to local people as possible. Curates of the day, with a hundred a year and a family to keep, were offered gifts from time to time and accepted them as legitimate recognition of their position. Head Constable Rogers simply adopted the same philosophy.

One of the stories told about him concerned a man whose sow gave birth to a litter, one of which was offered to the Head Constable. The gift was accepted but not immediately collected. A reminder was duly sent with the message that the porker was grown to the point where it no longer relied on maternal nourishment and had developed a healthy appetite for barley meal. The gift was still not called for and references to the extremely healthy appetite of the animal became the norm with each renewed reminder. The gift was eventually collected but not until the 'healthy appetite' had availed the animal of eight stones of additional flesh.

Another story concerned an anonymous sack of potatoes addressed simply to 'Rogers'. It was accepted as though it had been handed over personally. The contents had been half consumed when the Rogers, the man for whom the potatoes had really been intended, turned up to claim them.

What was to be done? The official Rogers, he who ran the law in the town, had consumed half of another's property. He said that had a crime been committed he could lock himself up and in due course appear in the witness box to give evidence against himself, but he was sure there would be no conviction. The sender of the spuds was clearly to blame, having addressed them less than carefully enough. The official Rogers came out on top of the discussion with the unofficial Rogers, who was persuaded to forego the consumed items without further complaint and, in addition, be donor of the remaining half.

Another story came from the man himself when he spoke at the dinner following the re-election of Mayor Beasley in 1874. It told of the time the Head Constable stopped a man on Reffells Bridge who had suspicious bulge under his coat. The bulge turned out to be a hare and was confiscated as being held in less than lawful possession and the man was asked his address. 'Walton-on-the-Hill' was the answer. Rogers told the man to get off home and look out for a summons for the offence. A boy was sent with the hare to the police station, which was where the Rogers family lived, with instructions to place it into the hand of Mrs Rogers.

But the suspect's address was incomplete. George was unable to summons a man who, through his own laxity he could not locate, and as the hare would not have lasted a week...... Here a hand was placed upon a portly paunch and the assembled guests knew precisely where the hare went.

E.Harcourt Burrage relates not just these stories but also rounds up the opinions of those who knew the Head Constable to show us that he was a man at ease with his position and at a level with the public. Often, he says, backsliders of small misdemeanour were treated to a 'Now, now, this sort of thing just won't do' shake of the head that was enough to set them back on the straight and narrow, whilst dealing with those of less persuadable disposition with considerably greater sterness indeed.

Was Head Constable George Rogers a figure of his time who perhaps would not have survived so successfully in a different period of our history? It sounds as though he was adaptable to any era, but if not the fact that he was perfectly suited to his own seems beyond doubt.

The Fire Brigade

Basic fire protection depends on two things, a water supply and the ability to deliver that water to the seat of any unwanted fire. Up to and around 1800 this was achieved in Reigate by water piped from the castle moat to the cage (prison) in the centre of the town, and delivered to an outbreak of fire by buckets, perhaps a water cart, and man power.

When the cage was demolished this facility was lost but in 1809 Lords Somers and Hardwicke donated two manual fire engines to the Old Borough. On the 8th of November of that year, at a vestry held to make a rate for the relief of the poor, consideration was given to,

'the necessity of appointing proper persons to work and keep in use the fire engines now deposited in the Markit (sic) House of Reigate, the aforesaid being the gift of the Right Honourable John Lord Somers and the Right Honourable Philip Earl of Hardwicke, assisted by a small subscription from the Insurance Office, for the use of the inhabitants of the Parish of Reigate against any fire that might happen within the said Parish.'

It is interesting to note that the meeting was at the Rose and Crown, an inn at 42-44 High Street, Reigate, dating from around 1700, and disappearing around 1900. At the same meeting it was also resolved,

'that when the above persons are called out they shall receive five shillings each person for each time as the said engines are wanted in order to keep them in use as aforesaid.'

These engines were horse-drawn pumps with hoses, and had wooden handles each side to manually pump water drawn from a local pond or stream. The men elected to 'work' the engines were presumably also responsible for getting an engine to any fire and recruiting local manpower to do the pumping under their direction.

It was also resolved, *'that all expenses attending the said engines and the keeping in use the same to be paid by the Borough and Foreign in equal proportions.'* Population was mainly centred around the Old Borough, which comprised the 400 acres of Reigate town, and as the fire engines were both kept in the Old Borough it must have required relatively little time to deal with a fire there compared with the travelling time to the sparsely populated acres of the Foreign. Because the population was also so much denser in the Old Borough it might be assumed that the majority of the calls would be to there. It would appear, therefore, that the Old Borough was getting its fire needs subsidised by the Foreign.

With the emergence of the new community to the east there was a call for one of Reigate's two engines to be housed in the Foreign, presumably at Warwick Town. It seems that this call went unheeded, but after incorporation the new Council decided to take over control of the Old Borough's fire brigade. According to a history of the brigade written in the 1930s, a notice was sent out in November, 1864, to fire brigade members requiring them to hand over the fire engine, their uniforms and accoutrements. They apparently refused, saying that they were not appointed by the new-fangled Corporation, nor had the existing engine been supplied by it. It seems that they woke up one day soon after this to find that the door of the engine house had been forced and the engine put under lock and key elsewhere. The Corporation announced that it was forming a new Reigate brigade under the captaincy of Mr J.H.Apted and issued a notice inviting men to apply for posts. Some of the members of the previously existing brigade joined the new one, among them Edwin Legg, son of the previous captain.

At this time there was still just the one brigade, although the question of a second force soon arose. At a meeting of townsmen at the Tower Inn, Redhill, on 18th April, 1865, the decision was taken to inaugurate such a force, to be called 'The Redhill Volunteer Fire Brigade.' The personnel were to consist of four officers and at least eight firemen, who were:

Superintendent	Mr Levi Collins
Secretary	Josias Markwick
Foreman	William Fuller
Engineer	Mr Wilkinson
Sub-engineer	Mr Elmslie
Firemen	Mr Mulley
	Mr Edward Lambert
	Mr Robins
	Richard Bailey
	Mr I. G. Sanders
	Mr F. Coluom (sic)
	Mr Topliss

There had to be a permanent home for the new town's fire engine and in a motion proposed by Councillor Young at a Council meeting of 9th September, 1865, it was proposed, '*that the Watch Committee be empowered to carry into effect their recommendation as to a watch house and lock-up cells at Warwick Town to include a shed for the fire engines and water carts at a cost not to exceed £400.*' A proper police station in the town had not yet been built but a new watch house and cells rectified this situation and the opportunity was being taken to house the fire engine at the same time.

The original 1809 engines needed replacement in 1857 and 1865, but even new manual engines, and the procedures of their operation, suffered from several limitations. One was that there was nearly always a delay between the notification of a fire and the arrival of the volunteer firemen at the station, as they had to be called out from home or work, and also of the horses which had to be provided from a field or livery stables.

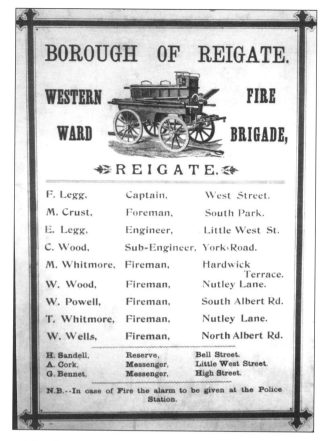

The Borough was originally divided into two wards. Before the two brigades were amalgamated in 1909 the Reigate brigade served the Western Ward and the Redhill brigade the Eastern Ward. This poster of a hundred years ago shows a typical manual engine of the type then used.
(Picture courtesy Sherry Legg)

This was partially overcome with the purchase of the first motorised engine in 1914. The first use of the 1914 engine was at the Athenaeum fire in the Brighton Road, Redhill, in 1915.

Another limitation of the manual engines was that the operation of them was hard, physical labour. This latter might have been overcome by the purchase of a steam powered engine in 1897, of which there was a trial by the brook in the Market Field, but the purchase was not proceeded with because, according to the Mayor of the time, there was nowhere to house it. Again, motorization solved the problem. The manual engines remained in parallel use until 1924.

Reigate got a new fire station at the Municipal Buildings in 1902, which was the year after the Borough's most notable fire at Nicol's store in the centre of Redhill, when two assistants lost their lives and the brand new building was destroyed. Both brigades fought the fire and the Croydon brigade also attended, with one of their horses collapsing and dying after the hard gallop to Redhill.

There continued to be a brigade for each of the towns, both of them under the control of the Council but each under its own Superintendent (or Captain) until it was decided in the name of more efficiency to amalgamate them and the out-stations at Meadvale, South Park and Earlswood, under a single Chief Officer. This occurred in 1909 when Major Rouse was appointed Chief Officer and the captains of the time became his superintendents.

Reigate had been provided with a new fire station at the Municipal Buildings in 1902 but Redhill had to wait until 1931 for its new station in London Road.

In 1938/9, when war appeared imminent, local authorities funded by Government recruited auxiliary firemen and women as a part of their local brigades. When war was declared many became full-timers, others remained part-time. The air raids by the Luftwaffe made it clear that there was a need for standardisation within the fire service, and the Government formed the National Fire Service (NFS) in 1941, when all brigades were absorbed into one national force. This was the end of the Reigate Borough Fire Brigade, although the Government promised that the service would return to local government control after the war. When this happened in 1948 brigades returned to County control, not borough control as before, although some county boroughs, such as Croydon,

A notable fire was that at Gatton Hall in 1934. Here a fireman inspects the remains of the marble hall as smoke and steam rise around him in a moody and sombre record of the fire's destructive aftermath. (Picture courtesy Jack Sales)

were designated as fire authorities.

With the 1948 denationalisation of the NFS most counties were able to simply take over the existing control structure as it was. Surrey's situation was different because it had the problem that its brigades had been controlled by two regional HQs and three Fire Force HQs, with the consequence that there was no single centralised HQ from which to organise its brigades. In 1952 the idea of setting up a new HQ at St. David's at Reigate was first aired publicly. Incorporated in the scheme was a plan to replace the stations at Redhill and Reigate with a single station.

The following year the idea was given

substance by the Minister of Housing and Local Government when he announced that he had approved the purchase order for the property. There was opposition to the idea but St. David's became operational as the Surrey Fire Brigade HQ in October of 1955, with Redhill and Reigate fire stations closing at their respective sites and combining at St David's two months later. When opened there was also a tactical training centre, where preparation for the kind of fires that might be caused in an atomic war was carried out. This was a Home Office operation which was closed at St. David's and moved elsewhere in 1957.

Fire at the Athenaeum Works, Brighton Road, 1915, which was the first serious turn-out for the Borough's new motorised engine.

An escape ladder mounted on an early, solid tyred vehicle outside the Reigate Fire Station.

Redhill Life and Times 1880 - 1899

Roads and Traders

In 1882 a letter appeared in the Surrey Mirror complaining about the muddy state of Cromwell Road and the fact that heavy traffic used it to avoid the hill of Station Road. This 'hill' by today's standards is no more than a gradual rise from the town centre to St Matthew's Church, but for heavily laden carts drawn by a single horse must have been worth the detour, mud or no mud.

A subsequent letter pointed out that Cromwell Road had not yet been adopted by the authorities so any repairs would be at residents' cost, and it also had some complaints of its own. It said that there were brilliant lights in Reigate at the Town Hall and Market Place, but none at the Red Cross nor any in Redhill opposite the Rev. Gosse at the Somers Arms (now the Firs, Brighton Road) or at Frenches Corner. The writer also wanted better road surfacing, such as tar paving plus kerbing, and said he had thought that when the drainage work was finished the roads would have been improved, but nothing had happened.

The Surrey Mirror editor had extra information, as he noted that additional lamps had been ordered for some of the places mentioned and said that the subject of Cromwell Road was to be looked into.

There is a small puzzle here, and that is why the Rev. Gosse's abode was referred to as the Somers Arms in 1882 when it had ceased to be that forty years before at the end of the old coaching days. Perhaps the Somers Arms name lingered locally in spite of having been transferred to the beer house at Reffells Bridge.

Tradesmen were still carrying on business in Redhill much as they had done since the very earliest days of the town. J.G.Marriage and Sons were delivering new milk from Ham Farm dairy, Redhill, at 4d per quart and offering milk from the same cow for infants and invalids if required. Other traders included R.Caffyn, tailor and habit maker, of Station Road; W.H.Cook, builder, undertaker and monumental mason also of Station Road, and William Berrett, who, next door to Jennings' High Street shop, was now in his 17th year of business, selling, *'the cheapest drapery goods, dress goods, mantles, costumes, carpets, boots and shoes.'*

R.Nicol sold all sorts of clothes at his establishment opposite the station in the years before the Market Field was developed with shops and he moved into brand new premises on the corner of Station Road and the High Street. E.S.Lambert, tailor, hatter and general outfitter, still carried on business at 5, Station Road in a business established in 1857.

Thomas Gundry was offering a comprehensive range of brewed liquids at prices that might make us envious of his customers, but probably the truth is that the prices then were the equivalent of those paid today. Were we able to travel back in time we might benefit, but had we to make a living then we would more than likely be viewing prices in a different light.

THOMAS GUNDRY
Warwick Brewery
STATION ROAD, REDHILL

	Firkin (9 gals)	Kild (18 gals)	Brl (36 gals)
Mild Ale	9/-	18/-	36/-
Family Bitter*	9/-	18/-	36/-
Family Ale	10/6	21/-	42/-
Mild Family Ale	10/6	21/-	42/-
Pale Ale	12/-	24/-	48/-
India Pale Ale	13/6	27/-	54/-
Stock Ale	13/6	27/-	54/-
Porter	9/-	18/-	36/-
Single Stout	11/3	22/6	45/-
Double Stout	13/6	27/-	54/-

*N.B. - Highly Recommended

1882 advertisement
Prices were rising and although beer prices of the time, plus gin and rum at 12/- and 15/- per gallon, with whiskey 18/- per gallon, might look ridiculously cheap by modern standards, they were dear enough for a time when the rentals of property had risen 42% on average between 1852 and 1882.

A Court for Redhill

For a long time there had been pressure for a petty sessions courthouse to be set up in Redhill so that people from the town did not have to face the inconvenience and expense of travelling to the Reigate court. Permission for such a courthouse in Redhill was granted to the Council by Government in 1882 but there had already been a history of some desire to move partly away from Reigate sessions. In 1870 the Council had leased a house in Redhill High Street from Mr C.J.Smith for minor cases, and in November, 1881, had arranged with the Market Hall Company to use its hall, although this was not done. Reigate's Public Hall had for a time been used but found inconvenient due to lack of space. Magistrates had used the Old Town Hall from 1877 to 1880 after Lord Somers spent £400 making the building more fitting for the job, the building being his property.

By the 1880s the people in the eastern side of the Borough still wanted half of the cases heard in Redhill, especially those that arose there. Airing of the subject continued, with the Council discussing whether Reigate and Redhill should both have courthouses but not coming to a decision. Argument against was that alternating court sessions between Reigate and Redhill would cause confusion, as visitors would not know which court to go to. Argument for was that Council meetings had always alternated between the towns and councillors were not confused, so why should Redhill be deprived of the facility?

It was also pointed out that the population of Redhill was twice that of Reigate and there was the expense of taking prisoners to Reigate (adding fuel to the charge that most of the crime being dealt with was committed in Redhill anyway). This was countered by the statement that if Redhill miscreants objected to travelling to Reigate then what about the mayor? - when he was from the east ward he had to travel.

Voting to use the Market Hall for the purpose of hearing cases was a problem for those Council members who were shareholders in Redhill Market Hall and therefore had a pecuniary interest, as the Market Hall Company would get rent for use of Hall for legal proceedings. The problem was put to the vote with inconclusive results amid criticism that a central magisterial premises should be provided. Later in the year the Council decided that the Old Town Hall would be used for the administration of justice and the Market Hall as a police court. What the difference was is unclear but the Redhill premises were still not used because the justices' clerks considered the appointment not to be legal, even though counsel's opinion was that the Council was empowered to appoint courts. This was made more or less irrelevant by the fact that the justices themselves decided the venue and always selected Reigate anyway.

This was no help to those from the east side of the Borough. On August 21st there were twenty-six cases heard; twenty-three from Redhill and just three from Reigate. Twelve were education cases and Redhill women with children had to wait all day to be heard. The argument in favour of a special day to be set aside for their cases to be heard in their own town seemed never stronger.

Mr Robert Field JP of Oxford Road, Redhill, Mayor of the Borough of Reigate from November 1881 to November 1884

It was at this time that the police purchased a set of photos of notorious criminals so they could be recognised should they venture into the Borough. A criminal of small notoriety, an inmate of the Farm School, was convicted of stealing a 2/- book from Mr Boorne of the High Street and sentenced to three months prison with hard labour, the Mayor, R.Field, on the bench.

If this seems harsh treatment then consider the case of tramp Arthur Roberts who met PC Woods dressed in plain clothes on Redstone Hill and asked him for a few pence. He was promptly arrested, taken into custody and received 7 days hard labour for begging. At least he was fed free of charge, which, we presume, was what he had been after in the first place.

Transport and Traction Engines

The case of the Doods footpath dominated the press for some time in 1882 when Mr A.Waterlow enclosed some of it, narrowing it where it crossed his property. The path was deemed to be old, the actual description used being, '*A certain strip of land used from a time whereof the memory of man runneth not to the contrary,*' and was adjudged a pleasant country walk. Certainly the path had its place in history, running from Reigate towards Redhill and possibly linking with the medieval path through Wiggie to parts beyond. In the end Mr Waterlow was forced to restore the path to its previous width of six to ten feet.

An alternative to taking the footpath was the new horse-drawn omnibus that was running between the two towns. It was apparently a successful venture, although less so on the day an axletree broke on the ascent of Grammar School Hill, partially upsetting the vehicle. The jolt would have also upset those riding inside, although on such a hill it was the practice for the conductor, and often passengers, to get out and walk beside

*Reigate to Redhill Horse Bus
(Courtesy Surrey Mirror)*

used to one then they would become used to the other. Attempts had been made via the by-laws to get traction engines banned from the highways between 10am and 6pm, but without success.

Shops, Pub Hours and Road Names

Shop hours had been reduced in 1878 and shops now closed at 5pm on Wednesdays and 7pm every other day. Shopkeepers had never been happy with these shortened hours and were considering a return to 7pm every night.

This did not mean that the shop assistants got away at 7pm as there was still work to be done, but the shopkeepers claimed that assistants were away by 8pm. A letter in the local paper, signed simply *A Grocer's Assistant*, claimed, *'In closing at 5 it is scramble and muddle all day, and when the shop is closed would beg to suggest that we close at 7pm all year round and at 6pm on Wednesday in summer months. You said that if we close at 7 we get away at 8; this is not the case, unless something very special happens we can always get off by a quarter past eight at the latest.'*

This would seem to be a put up job, appearing in advance of a tradesmen's meeting on the subject, with the letter either being written under duress or not written by anyone who was ever a grocer's assistant. Evidence of this is other letters that appeared in the local press from assistants detailing hours between 5.30am, when they had to rise to get to work, and 11pm when they sometimes finished. These might have been the extremes but considering that they worked Saturdays and some Sundays, assistants' lives were not ones where leisure figured high on their agendas, much as they might liked it to have done.

the vehicle. In the age before motorisation the owner's name had to be painted on all carts and carriages with fines levied on those not complying.

One particular aspect of the times has already been singled out as the horse, but another might well be the quietness that prevailed in the absence of engines. This was not to last much longer and in fact was already being shattered in places by traction engines, about which people had been complaining for some time. These were becoming a part of the countryside, doing jobs that horses could not do. They were an offence to the ear, eye and nose and frightened horses, but then so had bicycles, which in their early days had been referred to as terror inspiring, and it was said that if horses could get

In April of 1882 the population of the Borough was put at 19,000 but the number of burgesses was 3,000, which meant that there were still 16,000 residents without the vote.

Redhill High Street in the mid 1880s. The Tower public house has since been rebuilt. Jennings' shop is on the left, just beyond the first blind. (Courtesy of Pamlim Prints)

The positive aspect of this was pointed out by the shopkeepers in saying that an assistant's half day off, when he got one, allowed so much time for recreation that it was highly appreciated - it's not difficult to see why.

At the eventual meeting of the Redhill tradesmen dealing with the matter of closing times were: W.Berrett; J.T. Sanders; H.Rowland; S.Gare; M.Wood; A.Wood; H.Trower; A.Trower; T.K.Pearce; T.A.Pick; F.Cliff; G.Shaw (grocer); Mr Fowler; Mr Potter; W.Pook; A.B.Boorne (bookshop); F.Strong; Mr Ellis; Mr Wood; G.Drury; Mr Lanaway; J.Benham; F.Hardy and Mr Horne. The outcome was that shops would continue to close at 5pm Wednesdays in summer months and 7pm the rest of the week. A separate meeting to decide shop times during winter would be held. A year later, in 1883, the working week for shop assistants remained at 68 hours, with four bank holidays off plus 7-10 days holiday.

The British Workman Coffee Tavern in the High Street (later Mutton's Hotel) opened 5am to 10pm and provided lodging rooms, meeting rooms, parties and lunches. It was a temperance establishment providing an alternative to alcohol. The first temperance meeting in England had been held in 1830 and there had been many since, including one at Redhill in February, 1882, which had been an attempt to stop the drunkenness caused by the sale of liquor on Sundays. Public Houses had been closed on Sunday mornings since 1849 and plenty of publicans attended the meeting to try to stop the loss of more trade.

Two firsts for Redhill in 1882 were the sound of a church bell from St Joseph's in the High Street and post indicators on the letter boxes so collection times could be seen. The names of a number of roads were changed around this time because there were others - sometimes two or three - with the same name. Gatton Road was changed to Grove Hill Road; Holmesdale Road (South Park) became St Luke's Road; Holmesdale Road (Meadvale) was renamed Lower Road; Somers Road

(South Park) changed to Eastnor Road; and Warren Road (Meadvale) became Copse Road. At the same time the Town Clerk brought to Council's notice the fact that although the name Meadvale had been popularly in use for many years, its old name of Mead Hole was still used on notices in that area because it had never been changed legally. This was put right and the name Mead Hole was officially consigned to history.

Redhill Common

Sixteen acres of Redhill common had been safely secured for the use of Borough residents fifteen years before but the rights of the Earl Somers to dig for gravel there had been exercised by him for some time and was still vigorously pursued, with train loads of spoil being removed. The banks on the east side of the common close to Sandpit Road are evidence of the diggings and it can be seen that not only had great inroads been made into that part of the common but that the rest of it was under threat.

There were those to whom the word 'spoil' applied to not just what was being removed from the common but also what was being done to it. They conceded that the Lord had the right to the gravel but pointed out that the commoners had equal rights to the herbage, and queried whether the Lord had the right to destroy one by removing the other. They began to collect evidence and take steps towards testing the right of Earl Somers to remove gravel.

The man mainly involved was Mr Samuel Barrow of Linkfield Street, owner of the Tannery. He commenced action in Her Majesty's High Court of Justice on 26th June, 1882. The result was the following agreement, dated 2nd March 1883, between Earl Somers and Messrs S.Barrow and W.B.Waterlow as to the proposed regulation of Redhill Common:

The parties (Barrow and Waterlow) to pay Earl Somers £3,000 plus costs.
1. In consideration Earl Somers will not dig, or allow to be dug or carried away, clay, sand or other materials from Redhill Common.
2. Mssrs Barrow and Waterlow to apply to competent authority for Redhill and Earlswood Commons to be protected and preserved for the recreation of the local inhabitants.
3. Earl Somers still entitled to compensation if land taken by Railway Company or any other Company.
4. William Brown (at Meadvale) and Thomas Williams (at Earlswood) still to be allowed to dig clay for brickworks but restricted to existing workings for as long as their brickworks continue, licences ceasing upon sale of brickyards.

Of the £3,000 that was paid to Lord Somers £1,000 was paid by Samuel Barrow, £1,000 by Walter Waterlow and £1,000 by the Corporation. For the purposes of improvement the Corporation provided an additional £2,000 plus £150 per year for maintenance. This expenditure was a contentious issue in Council because the commons lay in the east of the Borough, so it was natural for all of the east ward Councillors to be in favour of the planned expenditure but for 11 of the 12 in the west ward to be against. The vote was enough to carry the proposal by a majority of one, however. A provisional order was prepared by the Land Commissioners for England and later embodied in a Special Act of Parliament entitled 'Commons Regulation (Redhill and Earlswood Commons) Provisional Order Confirmation Act, 1884.'

Samuel Barrow and Walter Waterlow did the Borough a great favour, for not only was the digging stopped but as a result of item 3 a conservation body was set up for the common, improvements made and the common looked after for many years.

The agreement allowed for each of the large landowners in the Borough, Lord Somers, Lord Monson and Walter Blanford Waterlow (who had supported Samuel Barrow) for his lifetime to appoint one conservator, with one being appointed by the Lord of the Manor for the time being, one by the Commissioner of HM Works and Public Buildings, and six by the local Council. This made eleven in all, but after the lifetimes of the first three named there would be only eight.

The first conservators were Thomas Radford Hope of Redhill, nominated by HM Office of Works and Public Buildings; Walter Blanford Waterlow of 'High Trees', Redhill, nominated by himself; William John, 7th Baron Monson, nominated by himself; Samuel Barrow, 'Lorne House', Redhill, nominated by himself; and Thomas Vernon Somers Cocks, nominated by the successors of Lord Somers, deceased. The Council representatives were Alderman Robert Field (then Mayor), Henry Austen, George Edwin Pym, Henry Summers, Charles Joseph Smith and Councillor William Brown (the same William Brown

William Brown, owner of the Meadvale Brickworks and Mayor 1893-5

mentioned in the agreement who had the brickworks at Meadvale). Clair Grece was the Clerk. Work carried out by the Conservators included new paths, tree planting, especially the Jubilee plantation at the top of the common and the Diamond Jubilee clump near the gates leading to High Trees (see p137/8), and the construction of the upper lake on Earlswood Common. Also the reconstruction and enrichment of the undercliff after a design by Mr Richard Peat of Meadvale (adjudged the best of six submitted). In 1884 the common alongside Mill Street was laid out as a pleasure gardens as part of the programme of improvements to the common carried out by the new Commons Conservators.

The body of Common Conservators no longer exists and the common is far less attended to today, with much of it returning to woodland.

Schools, Health and Post

Burglaries in the Borough were increasing to the point where it was necessary for two extra policemen to

Samuel Barrow
(Courtesy Reigate and Banstead Council)

be taken on and extra lighting to be considered. This was a social downturn from which no doubt all kinds of inferences could be drawn, but there was no doubt about the inference to be drawn early in 1883 at a meeting at Warwick Hall, Redhill, of the managers of the elementary schools in the neighbourhood. Her Majesty's Inspector of Schools had intimated that the school accommodation in various parts of the Borough was very defective and fell far short of requirements and steps needed to be taken to rectify matters. There was a large amount of accommodation but much of it needed considerable repair, and apart from that other schools were wanted. The choice was between the School Board previously mentioned and raising the required funds as follows:

St Luke's district (Sth Pk)   £1000
St John's   £2000
       £951 so far raised)
St Matthew's   £3500
       (£1500 so far raised)

There were also several important schools in the district besides the church schools and Mr Duncan of Reigate School said that Redhill school managers were in favour of a School Board, thinking that the present was a very good time to inaugurate one. He envisaged that religious education would be continued under a School Board and church school leaders should have no worries on the matter. He thought that however schools tried to raise money for their schools they would not stave off the eventual coming of a School Board.

Landscape artist Mr John Dakin of Bridge Road had two pictures accepted by the Royal Academy but unfortunately they were not hung due to lack of space.

Mr Waterlow agreed and proposed that the Town Council apply to the Education Department for a School Board. The Rev. Brass was against and, as not all school managers were present, a request was made for an adjournment of 2 weeks. The Mayor said that their absence was his fault as he had sent notices for distribution but had not had all the addresses. Mr Waterlow withdrew his motion and another meeting in May - the Market Hall's largest ever - voted to keep the present schools and avoid a School Board.

Under the old manorial system there had been an official called the Inspector of Nuisances in each of the petty boroughs. His job had been to see that all those situations where public health was put at risk were remedied, and his late 1800s successor was sometimes still known by the old title, at other times more modernly as the Inspector of Sanitation. The man in this job before 1884 had been Mr Job H. Apted, who in that year was succeeded by Mr Nimrod Walter. The job paid £50 per annum for about two days work, but the problem in the growing Borough was that the workload had increased to the point where it could not properly be carried out under such limitations.

Problems with public health frequently occurred. In 1893 there was a drought which caused wells to run dry. People used water from ponds as drinking water with the inevitable results. There was no isolation hospital, and charladies, upholsterers, laundresses, tailors, bootmakers, milk carriers and others with reason to go to people's homes continued to do so even when they had fever in their own homes, as to declare same and not visit meant loss of income. In 1895 there was an outbreak of smallpox in nearby rural areas, and in 1896 scarlet fever swept through the Borough during hot weather.

As if these were not difficulties enough for the Sanitary Inspector then extra workload imposed by the requirements of the Cow Sheds and Dairy Order, the Inspections of Bakehouses Order, the Infectious Diseases Notification Act of 1889, and the Workshops and Factories Act of 1896, plus by-laws pertaining to the accumulation of manure and slaughterhouse regulation, made life impossible for him.

And he said so a number of times over the years. He had assistants who left him because they could earn more than he was able to pay from his £50 p.a. and in 1896 things came to a head and he resigned. In a way this was a good thing for the Council as his contract had two years left to run and his departure relieved them of the decision of whether to pay him more or re-organise the sanitary department, which was what they did, appointing a new man and making the job full time.

It is an 1880s winter day around noon. Two men stand in conversation in the middle of Redhill crossroads with traffic levels low enough to allow them to be there fairly safely. The horse trough now stands at Shaws Corner and the Wheatsheaf public house has since been rebuilt and renamed. The building to the right has also been rebuilt and is now Lloyds Bank. The left foreground, the north west corner of the Market Field, has since been built on, and the only familiar features are those buildings to be seen on the north side of Station Road as it stretches away towards the spire of St Matthew's Church.
(Courtesy Pamlim Prints)

The centre of old Redhill from a slightly different angle. The date is approximately 1885-1895. On the left is the Market Field again, and in the distance the building, now Lloyds Bank, which then housed Lambert's butchers' shop. To its right is the Globe Building where Barton & Co., Wine Merchants, carried on their business (the drawing of Barton's premises, right, shows it in much more detail). The block of shops on the right of the above picture stretched from the Market Hall to the South Eastern Hotel on the corner of Ladbroke Road. The furthest shop is Pearce's printers; next was Harrie Stacey's premises (before he moved across the road) with solicitors Morrison and Nightingale above. John Robinson, boot maker, was next, followed by the tobacco shop of William Rowland, established around 1877. Saddler and harness maker, J.Sanders, had his shop next door, and is the last one to be seen here. The picture was probably used by him as an advertisement, looking as if it has been coloured, the shop name enhanced, and the words 'and at Horley' added between the upper windows.
(Picture courtesy Neil Ferrett)

Mr J.T.Sanders, owner of the saddlery in Station Road and a Borough Councillor for over twenty-five years.

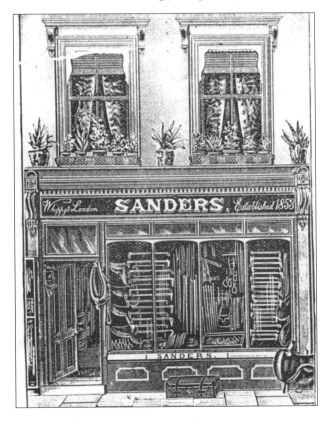

Mr Sanders' shop in 1892, looking much as it does in the photograph on the previous page.

Football and the Sports Ground

Although there are no local professional football clubs there are many amateur ones. Reigate Priory is the oldest, being first registered in 1804. Redhill FC was formed in 1894 and played at Wiggie for a number of years. One notable game on this ground was against the West London club of Queens Park Rangers in the 1895/6 season, which Redhill won 2-0 in the rain in front of a not unusual crowd of 200. Players were Batten, half back (scored); C.P.Murray, back; Rowlinson, another defender; Peskett in goal; Purkis, left half; W.P.Brown, right half; Power, outside right; Donaldson, outside left; Gilford, midfield, (scored); plus Stafford and Evans, forwards.

The adverse outcome of their last match of the 1896 season against Maidstone Invicta was not claimed to be due to unfairness, but it was pointed out that if the team had not had to endure a two and a half hour train journey on the crawling SE railway, followed by a walk of more than a mile (all uphill) and then a match on a pitch ten yards smaller all round than Wiggie, the 2-7 losing score-line might have been improved - and afterwards they still had to get home.

On 23rd June, 1896, the Redhill Sports Ground and Athletics Co. Ltd was formed with Henry Trower chairman. Its main asset was 9 acres fronting London Road, with tenants' and grazing rights either expired or bought up, although the company did not own the land outright. Its object was to promote the ideals of football and other sporting activities.

The 9 acres comprised rough ground described as little more than a swamp. Two streams through it had to be culverted, with trees cut and grubbed and the timber sold. A hedge on the London Road boundary was replaced by a park pale oak fence. The north boundary to land of Mrs Green was agreed, an entrance from Ladbroke Road was granted by Mr Trower, and a pavilion was to be erected. Cost of all works came to £3,500 raised in shares of £1. The work was completed within a year, only the proposed pavilion containing a cricket score box, a pavilion room, two dressing rooms and a store had still to be built. Redhill FC continued to play at Wiggie but with the possibility of transferring to the new ground.

Unfortunately the formation of the Sports Ground and Athletics Company coincided with a time when there was some dissension about the make-up of the football team. From 1895 some of the players had been amateurs of note from outside who were paid expenses to play for RFC. Payments had run the club into debt and there were those who felt that the team ought to use more local players. Conditions set for the team to transfer to the new ground included no expenses to be paid to players travelling to Redhill matches, for local men to be used whenever possible, and for the Sports Ground Committee to appoint the club

secretary and approve or disapprove the club's proceedings. These conditions were accepted by the club committee subject to a special meeting that was never called. Mr Diehl, the then club secretary said that there was a lack of local players of suitable quality and that he was in negotiations with seven or eight outside amateurs qualified as senior players, and he wanted permission to engage them at £4-5 per week overall. Permission was refused and he resigned.

There was an official opening of the Sports Ground in 1897 as part of Queen Victoria's Jubilee celebrations in the town, when the public was admitted to a sports meeting. The public was also admitted to subsequent football matches played there but the ground remained officially private. The ground did not become public until 1923 when Lord Monson agreed the sale of the acreage, an otherwise valuable site in almost the centre of the town, for £1,200, money raised by the War Memorial Committee.

The deeds were handed over and it

Seated on the front of the carriage at the 1897 opening of the Sports Ground is Mr Jeremiah Colman. In the body of the carriage are the Hon. Henry and the Hon. Mrs Cubitt. (Picture courtesy Surrey Mirror)

became the Memorial Sports Ground, left in trust for the people of the town and for the senior football club. Matches drew large Saturday afternoon crowds sometimes numbered in the thousands. It was not uncommon for the entrance queue to stretch back to the centre of the town, and when the game ended the crowd would spill out onto the main street, sometimes stopping the traffic between the ground and the Market Hall. The largest recorded attendance was 7,000 for the 1955 FA cup game against Hastings. There were 6,000 there to see the FA amateur cup game against Hendon in the early 1960s but even that massive support failed to help the Reds, who lost 0-6.

There was another team - Redhill Wednesday - which also used to play at the Memorial Ground. Organised by local traders at a Towers pub meeting in 1899 - shopkeepers were sure of Wednesday afternoon half day closing - the team enjoyed three golden seasons in 1928-31 during which they hardly lost a game and in each of those years won the same five competitions, the Surrey Midweek County Cup, the East Surrey Hospital Charity Cup, Croydon Midweek Charity Cup, Redhill Wednesday League and Croydon Wednesday League.

Redhill FC ceased to play at the Memorial Ground when the north-east quadrant was redeveloped in the late nineteen-seventies. A new venue was found for them at Kiln Brow. The stand at Redhill was demolished and a small part of the ground, where the terraces had been, was taken for the new town by-pass.

Queen Victoria's Jubilee

On Wednesday 23rd September, 1895, Queen Victoria became the longest serving British monarch. Two years later it was decided that Her Majesty's 60 years on the throne should be celebrated in Redhill in a practical way, the only problem being in deciding which of the

Cycling

Many activities took place at the Sports Ground, including cycle races. A number of clubs existed in the town and a new one, Redhill United Cycling Club, was formed in June, 1897, with its HQ at the Cyclist's Rest in London Road. The cyclists were frequently troubled by dogs and many carried an ammonia gun as a deterrent, although the effect was limited by problems of aiming and firing and staying on the bike at the same time. Nevertheless there was a move to ban the weapon due to the extreme agony caused to animals unfortunate enough to harry a cyclist skilled in its use.

suggestions put forward was the best one to adopt.

The most suitable seemed to be an addition to the Cottage Hospital but there was considerable support for a new rifle range for the Volunteer Force, which had lost its previous range at Reigate Hill in 1892. In the end both of these were realised. Other suggestions included the provision of an open space on Reigate Hill close to the suspension bridge, new almshouses and enlargement of the Literary Institute.

Several celebratory activities were staged. A treat for local children took place on a perfect June day at Mr Waterlow's estate at Great Doods, Reigate, and 450 old folk were treated to a sit-down dinner at the Market Hall. The new Redhill Sports Ground was used for the first time, as detailed previously, and there was a torchlight procession up to Redhill Common from where, it is said, at least 30 celebratory beacons could be seen blazing near and far. At Reigate there was a parade of cyclists on decorated machines.

A group of trees known as the Jubilee Plantation had been planted on Redhill

Common ten years earlier to mark the monarch's fiftieth year on the throne, and still stands on the east side of Redhill Top Common. A second clump was planted west of these, fifty-five trees being purchased at 2/6d each, and the ceremony was attended by most of the prominent people of the day. Both groups of trees have suffered from violent weather, especially the 1987 storm, and fences around them have long since disappeared.

Trees also figured heavily in plans to beautify Redhill town by planting them along the streets. Prominent townsmen formed a committee and planting commenced in the 1897 autumn. Many postcards of the town show trees adorning various streets and forecourts but none remain, having fallen victim of road widening and other development, although trees have since been planted in Station Road in 1977 and are gradually reappearing in other parts of the town.

Improvement of the town was carried out by the planting of trees in many of the streets. The money was raised by a committee of prominent townsmen and planting commenced in 1897. This 1907 card shows London Road and the sender has put a cross on the card to mark the house in which she was staying but notes on the back that the trees partly hide it. The picture also shows the Colman Institute, with a pair of tall lamps outside, and the wooden fence that then closed the Sports Ground off from view of the main road.

Committee for Planting Trees in the main thoroughfares of Redhill.

Chairman
MAJOR KINGSLEY O. FOSTER, J.P.

Hon. Treasurer
ARTHUR TROWER, Wiggie, Redhill.

Hon. Secretary
HENRY SEWILL, The Old Rosary, Redhill

Chairman of Executive Committee
GEORGE LAKER

Executive Committee
ALDERMAN J.T. SANDERS, COUNCILLORS G.R.HUNT, AND HENRY TROWER, MESSRS A. MEIER, R.B. VIALL, E.G. FIELD, A. WOOD, M. WOOD, T.R .HOOPER, W.H. FOWLER, A.C. MUTTON, W. ROSE, F.C.MAITLAND, F.H. ELLWOOD, R. ADAMS, R.W. ROBINSON, HY. LIBBY, T.PADWICK, C.H. FARBROTHER, H.J. STEVENS, T. BACON PHILLIPS, W. POOK, E.J. HAMNETT, T. LEACH, F.A. MONK, W. HANDSCOMBE, R.S. NICOL.

The question of improving the appearance of Redhill Town having been for some time under discussion, a Committee was formed to examine into the matter. The Committee reported that since extensive rebuilding in architectural styles was not to be speedily expected, the only available means of improvement seemed to be the systematic planting of trees and shrubs wherever possible.

The improving effect of trees and shrubs can now be observed at the few spots where planting has been already done in the main thoroughfares, and many roads in the Borough have been rendered beautiful by this simple means alone.

A public meeting having been called on July 21st, a large representative general committee was formed to carry out a scheme which had been formulated by a preliminary committee.

The Executive Committee are glad to state they have gained the sanction of the Town Council, of the South Eastern Railway Company, and of the Redhill Gas Company, as well as of many private owners, for plantation of the chief thoroughfares and enclosing bordering lands, and of paths and forecourts, under their control. A fund has been opened and subscriptions sufficient to warrant immediate commencement of the work have been promised.

The Executive Committee now appeal for contributions which may enable them to carry out the whole scheme during the present planting season. The scheme will at once make Redhill more pleasant to dwellers within and more attractive to RESIDENTS around the town, and therefore cannot fail to prove beneficial to TRADESMEN AND MEN OF BUSINESS. The improvement must also INCREASE THE VALUE OF PROPERTY, which now is undoubtedly depreciated by the unattractive appearance of the town, especially in the vicinity of the railway junction.

Contributions may be paid to the account of "Tree Planting Fund" at the London and County Bank, Redhill and Reigate, or to any member of the Executive Committee, or may be sent by cheque, post office order, or stamps, to the Hon. Treasurer, Arthur Trower, Wiggie, Redhill.

Collector: - J.R.BENHAM   92, Earlsbrook Road, Redhill.

More About the Commons

The Roundabout, a group of cottages about two hundred yards back from Pendleton Road south-west of the lakes, already mentioned in this history, once had no single access way to it for horses and carts, a feature shared by the sewage works, to which traffic from Woodhatch cut across the common before Woodhatch Road was made. Concern was expressed in 1897 at the disfigurement caused to the common in both cases and the remedy was channels cut into the grass so a single route was used and multiple tracks eliminated.

Another concern about use of the common arose when Mr Gillham asked for permission to hold meetings of the Safeguard of Redhill Good Lodge of Templars at night on ground adjacent to Mill Street, a patch also used by the Gospel Temperance Society and the Salvation Army. The chairman of the Commons Conservators said he had no knowledge of previous grants made, and committee member Mr Brooks was quite opposed to the granting of the request, arguing that once one group had permission it was hard to stop others. The common was for the enjoyment of the public, not for the haranguing of either a meeting or a mob. It was a nuisance that these people should go there and make a noise.

In spite of his objections the Conservators granted permission so long as local residents did not complain.

Other Matters

The Church Lads Brigade, formed in 1894, was associated with St Matthew's Church and used the parish rooms in the High Street as its base. It reached its diamond jubilee in 1954 but not its centenary, being disbanded in 1988.

The two electoral wards, Reigate East and Reigate West, which had existed since incorporation in 1863, became six in 1896.

There was disagreement over the new boundaries as being unfair to the more populated and expanding East Ward as the wards now became the East, South-East, Central, North, South-West and South. Each was preceded by the word 'Reigate', a practice that has continued until the present day. A current proposal to give names which more properly describes their location, such as Merstham, or Woodhatch, may be adopted in the near future.

At about the same time the Loop Line construction began badly with a ganger, John Williams, buried under 30 tons of earth and killed during the new Merstham tunnel excavations.

The Inaugural Car Run

This period was still the age of the train but it was also well into the beginning of that of the motor car. Little more evidence of this was needed than when, on November 14th, 1896, the Inaugural Motor Car Run through the Borough took place. It was an event described as: - 'an 'invasion' of specimens of horseless carriages, which may or may not become the popular vehicle of the future.'

Originally the cars were to make their way to the White Hart Hotel, Reigate, the old coaching hostelry where lunch was provided, without passing through Redhill, but at the last moment a decision was taken to change the route. The night before the run the Head Constable, Mr Metcalfe, issued a handbill informing inhabitants that cars would enter the Borough by way of London Road, Redhill, and proceed along Station Road to Reigate.

Fifty-four vehicles were listed and by noon a crowd had gathered at the centre of the town. It gradually increased to several hundred and the pavements of London and Station Roads were densely packed. Shortly after half past twelve the waiting crowd witnessed the arrival of a motor vehicle which entered Redhill at a rate which could have been little less than the

This Canstatt-Daimler was one of the 'popular vehicles of the future' referred to by the Surrey Mirror in November, 1896. It had taken part in the inaugural run and is pictured at the White Hart, Reigate, on the Tuesday after the run on its return journey to London. The occupant's identities are unknown.

regulation 14 mph

The unmetalled roads were very soft but Station Road corner, always awkward to vehicular traffic, was safely negotiated, although even at that speed there was some sliding in the mud. From noon there had been a continuous stream of cyclists, one of whom amused the crowd by coming a cropper at the corner. More cars came through but to the disappointment of the waiting crowd most cars stuck to the original route and entered Reigate without at all touching the eastern part of the Borough.

Reigate Market Square was decorated for the occasion. The lamp in the centre of the square was draped and crowned with a trophy of flags. Banners waved from the windows of the Constitutional Club, the Swan Hotel and the White Hart Hotel, while many of the townspeople and private residents sported bunting and other kinds of house decoration.

A large crowd of people assembled, while the gathering of carriages and cyclists was also very great. The police made every effort to keep the course clear as motors arrived at intervals of 10 minutes, cars and occupants being liberally bespattered with mud. Every window in the square was crowded with sightseers, whilst almost every other window possessed its photographer - amateur or otherwise.

Some Other Schools

An 1896 advert for a Boys Preparatory School at Radnor House, Station Road, Redhill, offered a boarding and day school at which boys were, *'carefully grounded and prepared for the Public Schools and examinations. Classes for carpentry and Drilling.'* The principal was Miss Johns, successor to Misses Clarke and Nettlefold. The Elmside School at the Common, Redhill, established 1891, principal Mr. T.Bundock BA, was also advertising vacancies for boarders, and the Redhill School of Music, 45 Station Road, Redhill, President Sir A.C. McKenzie invited those interested to get a prospectus and all information from Mr Arthur Wood, 45 Station Road. The population of the Borough was now 24,000 and no doubt there was a need for ever-increasing opportunities of all kinds in the town.

Tramways, Trippers and Strikers

There was a proposal for a tramway to be built from Merstham through Redhill to Earlswood Station, and from

The November, 1896, scene in Church Street, Reigate, as a car approaches the centre of the town, possibly not one which made the journey via Redhill. A title given to the event was 'The Emancipation Run', referring to the fact that the Locomotives On Highways Act 1896 removed the need for a man on foot to precede any motor vehicle, and raised the speed limit from 4 to 14mph, although Local Government Boards were empowered to reduce it, which they did to 12mph.
(Picture courtesy Eric Parsons)

The above picture of the east side of London Road dates from around 1890. Some of the buildings began as private houses and were converted to shops, the only one left as a house being next to William Rose's florist shop. (Pictures this and top of next page courtesy Neil Ferrett)

A. MEIER, CARRIAGE FACTORY (ESTABLISHED 1864)
LADBROKE ROAD, REDHILL
(OPPOSITE STATION)

~~~~~~~~~~~~~~~~~~~~~~~~~~~~~~~~~~~~

CARRIAGES of every description Built to Order, at the Lowest Possible Prices.
Elegance, combined with durability, guaranteed.

REPAIRS EXECUTED AT THE SHORTEST NOTICE   ESTIMATES GIVEN

~~~~~~~~~~~~~~~~~~~~~~~~~~~~~

Carriage designs of the Newest Styles may be viewed at the premises

<<<<<< Previous Page - *A busy Brighton Road, with people possibly having just left church. The Alderney Dairy on the right has the Britannia public house beyond it, the framework of a gasometer at the gasworks site sticking up above its roof. The Reading Arch is still an arch, and the spire of St Joseph's Church is visible, so the picture seems to date to between 1898 and 1902. The Chapel Road Congregational Church is also to be seen, and the two largest buildings on the left are the Methodist Church and the Athenaeum. On the very left is the studio and house of Dann and Sons, photographers. Two young ladies look out of an upper window and a man leans in the doorway - possibly Dann family members watching another member take the picture.*

In this view of the east side of London Road, Bailey and Luscombe, cabinet makers, occupy what was then the last building. Further down a woman in a white apron is outside the Sultan public house. Below is the front of the Sultan, with Linter's Cyclists' Rest next to it, a penny-farthing cycle wheel over its door and George Linter in straw hat in the doorway. The bicycles displayed were sold in the shop. Linter's had shops on both sides of the Sultan but would move into premises later built on the end of this row. (Lower picture courtesy John Eede)

In 1896 Mr Albert Makovski went into partnership with Mr Tamplin in London and Redhill. Their Redhill premises were in the Brighton Road and are pictured above. They were agents for Dennis Brothers of Guildford, and two of the cars are of this make, the other is a French Decauville. The fourth vehicle, partly hidden behind the others, is a very early electric mail van. It is said it was used to carry mail from Redhill post office to London nightly but would use up all its charge on the journey and have to be horse drawn back up the Brighton Road to Tamplin and Makovski for its recharge. (Other opinion is that it would have been unlikely to be able to travel so far on only one charge) The company later relocated to Reigate, and their old building at 58, Brighton Road, as it was in May, 1998, is pictured right.

Mr Albert Waterlow Makovski

Dr Hallowes died at his home in Station Road, Redhill, in 1897. He came to Reigate around 1865 as assistant to Dr Peter Martin and later became a partner in the firm of Holman and Waters and came to Redhill. He was Vice Chairman of Redhill Gas Co. The death also occurred, in August 1897, in Switzerland, of Mr E.F.Gedge, one-time councillor of the Borough. A granite water fountain in his memory was placed at Shaws Corner by the congregation of St Matthew's Church in memory of his many years as a churchwarden. It was later moved to the common at Whitepost Hill when replaced by the war memorial.

Godstone through Bletchingley, Nutfield and Redhill to Reigate, the rails to be laid on the highways. It never came into being but it would have been interesting to see how it would have affected the bus services, and how the rail crossing of the two routes in Redhill would have been designed. A tramway was proposed again in 1899, this time between the towns. Station Road would have had to be widened and there were those who thought Reigate would be spoiled forever by 'a noisy nuisance', and the project met the same fate as in 1896/7.

A council meeting at Brighton raised the subject of the cheap tripper; the visitor who came down on a Sunday at reduced train fares and behaved in an imperfect way. There was talk of a petition to the railway companies to cease the practice of cheap fares after August 1st, 'so as to give the town a chance of receiving better visitors.' It was said that on any Sunday there were more drunks than on Jubilee day. The reply of the Mayor and others was that 'Arry and 'Arriet, the typical London cockney or coster fraternity, had as much right to come to the town as the rich, the local traders benefiting from both, and the police could deal with the drunks.

It was not only Londoners who went to Brighton of course, people from many towns north of Brighton made the journey to 'London-By-The-Sea' in the summer. From Redhill special trains were put on for parties of several hundred by local organisations such as the temperance movement, although it was not unknown for many, even on those trips, to be incapable of walking unassisted back to Brighton Station through being the worse for drink.

There was a strike of building workers in the Borough by men earning 8d per hour wanting 1d per hour increase plus union recognition. They also wanted working hours to be restricted to 56 per week in summer and 8 hours per day in winter, 1 hour's notice of termination, a tools lock-up and eating place to be provided at sites, and overtime rate improvements that included double time for Sundays and Christmas Day.

Before Christmas, beef and suet tenders were accepted by the workhouse from Mr Weller of Redhill (successor to Mr Stevens) at 7d/lb. As an additional treat the older male inmates got extra tobacco and the old ladies extra snuff.

The Co-op

A business that could have been mentioned earlier in this history is that of the Reigate Industrial and Providential Society, its beginnings being back in early 1861, before Incorporation. It was inspired by local food prices that were higher than they were seen to need to be, and a shop had been established by August of 1863 in Reigate. In Redhill the first shop was in the High Street, and later the Society moved to four adjacent shops at 6-12 Cromwell Road, and were certainly there by 1898.

In 1896 a new abattoir of the Reigate Industrial and Provident Society had been opened in Cromwell Road. The surprising thing about it was its size, being only thirteen feet by thirteen feet, yet having separate 'lairs' for oxen, sheep and pigs. Extremely functional in all respects there could have been little room inside for anything other than the slaughtering process, carcasses being removed outside fairly quickly and therefore subjected to sanitary conditions that fell far short of modern standards.

The Society was to merge with the South Suburban Co-operative Society in 1930. Soon there was a large department store on the corner of Redhill's London and Clarendon Roads in addition to the Reigate store, plus branches at Merstham and South Park. The Redhill store was demolished in the early 1980s.

Other shops of the day included Arthur Wood's Musical Warehouse, established in 1868. Mr Wood had at one time been the principal tuner to a well-known piano maker, serving his apprenticeship in the manufacture of the instrument, so it was a natural progression for him to go into the business for himself.

Carnel & Co. dealt in children's and gentlemen's clothes and tailoring. The shop was situated next to that of Mr Wood on the same side of Station Road as the Warwick Arms Hotel.

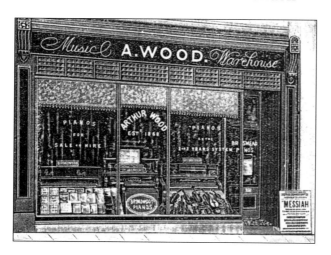

Wood's original premises at 41 Station Road.

Prize Fights

Prize fights took place in the town from time to time. In 1882 there was a fight for a purse of £20 between two men named Roberts and Bridge. Roberts threw in sponge after 11 rounds but both men were badly injured. The report of the incident stated that there was a large crowd with no intervention by police.

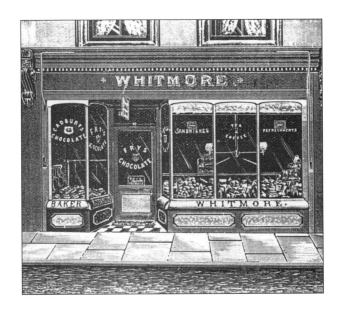

>>>>>>> *Shown top left of the **next page** are the premises of Mr T.H.Gooch, an oil, colour, varnish and hardware merchant. 'Colour' referred to the colouring for a base shade of paint, added to give the required colour before the days of ready-tinned paints in separate colours. The shop was situated on the very end of what later became known as Chandler's Alley, that narrow way once leading from the High Street to the railway station via a tunnel under the line but today much shortened and starting at the rear of the British Embassy night-club. The name was derived from later times when Gooch's shop became Chandler's fish and poultry shop, but perhaps it was once known as Gooch's Alley.*

Whitmore's shop was later Wapling's, and is shown below shortly before demolition, with almost a century between the pictures on this page.

Mr W.Whitmore's bakery shop (top left) was described in the 1891 business guide in the manner of the day, with the reference to class firmly included: - *'The business since it was started has developed into an extensive and ever-increasing trade, owing to the demand for Mr Whitmore's bread, which, on account of its general superiority to any other product in the neighbourhood, is increasing in demand amongst all classes in the town and neighbourhood.'*

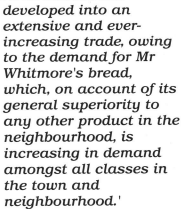

We can imagine the local housewife shopping for her family and standing in queue with a maid from a well-to-do family from the town sent for just one loaf, and the cook from a large country house on a twice or thrice weekly trip, arrived by train or trap, selecting bread and other bakery items.

Henry King's butcher's shop (above right) at Aberdeen House stood at the corner of Rees Road and Station Road West; the picture below shows the location more clearly. The 1891 Business Guide says the business was established fifty years before, which, if correct, could not have been by Mr King as he came originally from Bletchingley and acquired the business around 1867. He owned considerable property in the town, including the road on the south side of the Market Field, which led to a paddock by the brook. The junction of that road with the High Street was then known as King's Corner.

London Road, Redhill.

London Road, Redhill

A scene so different from that of the same place today, with not one feature remaining the same, giving us another example of the tree planting that achieved the purpose of beautifying the town. The Queen's Arms, partially hidden by the trees on the corner of Clarendon Road South, has now been replaced by the Sun on the opposite corner, and even that road name is changed to Queensway, with its direction altered and residential status dramatically changed to that of the main road of today. The Harlequin complex, with Sainsbury's supermarket beyond, dominates the current scene behind where the children on the right are standing. The Railway Bell public house is the first premises on the right, and is included in the sale notice on the following page.
(Sale notice courtesy Peter Hyder)

REDHILL, ○ SURREY.

FREEHOLD LICENSED & OTHER PROPERTY for INVESTMENT or ULTIMATE OCCUPATION.

Particulars and Conditions of Sale

OF THE VALUABLE

◁ FREEHOLD PROPERTY ▷

COMPRISING

FOUR SHOPS AND HOUSES,

INCLUDING THE

LICENSED PREMISES,

KNOWN AS

"THE RAILWAY BELL,"

AND BEING NOS.

2, 4, 6 & 8, LONDON ROAD,

(Formerly Nos. 1, 2, 3 & 4, Ladbroke Terrace),

REDHILL, ○ SURREY,

Occupying a magnificent business position in the heart of the town, adjacent to the Market Hall and other public buildings. The Property is let, partly on Lease, to old-standing tenants at low rentals amounting to £160 per annum, but is of the estimated present total rental value of

£170 per annum.

WHICH WILL BE SOLD BY AUCTION BY

Mr. J. S. RICHARDSON,

At the Mart, Tokenhouse Yard, City of London,

On WEDNESDAY, JUNE 29th, 1898,

At ONE o'clock precisely, in Separate Lots.

May be viewed by permission of the respective tenants and Particulars with Conditions of Sale obtained at the usual Hotels in the district; at the Auction Mart, London; and of

Messrs. J. & M. SOLOMON, Solicitors, 58, Finsbury Pavement, E.C.

Mr. J. S. RICHARDSON, Surveyor & Valuer, 50, Finsbury Square, E.C.

(Telephone No. 1,879 Avenue)

The Post Office

By 1884 there was a total of fourteen postal staff at Redhill, but considerable change was to take place in the organisation in the coming years. Postmaster Cole died in 1888 and was succeeded by Mr Bull in charge of both towns until Mr Dyer became Redhill Postmaster in July of 1890, when Mr Bull then became Postmaster of Reigate. The post office was transferred in 1891/2 from its Station Road site opposite St Matthew's, where it had been since 1856, to the Market Hall's new wing, and a sub post office that had been set up some years before at Jennings' in the High Street was closed.

Redhill became an important forwarding centre for mail for the area bounded by London, Reading and Dover, and the building of a large sorting office was begun at the station. The new facility opened in 1895. Two years later the free delivery to every house in the district was carried into effect, and by 1899 the fourteen post office staff of 1884 had become fifty-five.

The Town Clerk

As detailed in earlier chapters, the Town Clerk had taken part in the drive for Incorporation almost forty years earlier and at the end of the century he was still active in trying to see that manorial and parish functions, so far as they still existed, were amalgamated or aligned with Corporation practices. Vestry meetings to set a poor rate and see to matters affecting the burial board were still held, and Clair Grece was connected with them by being on various committees. He argued at many of these meetings that they were no longer properly constituted. A point in case was a vestry meeting of March, 1899, at the Market Hall, at which he got to his feet to tell members that not only had the meeting not been summoned by ministers or churchwardens but that it was not being held in a place where vestry meetings should be held. No doubt he was perfectly correct but a vote on the matter went against him and the meeting concluded its business. Perhaps his point of view was considered by others to be technically accurate but not warranting prevention of the business of the meeting being concluded.

The matter of court sessions at Redhill arose again in 1899. It seems not to have been dealt with since 1882 as comparisons were made in Council to the situation existing then, when there were 106 cases more from Redhill than from Reigate. Figures had since risen, the argument ran, to 185 cases more, so the need was heightened. In spite of this Reigate was still preferred by those whose votes counted the most, for a tied vote of 9-9 prompted the Mayor, who had not voted himself, to declare that the motion fell. The Surrey Mirror felt the need to comment, saying that it was hard to see why the matter was voted against as two thirds of the cases were from Redhill. It added that the vote was purely on party lines, and anyway, the decision was for the magistrates to decide, not the Council.

The court-in-Reigate-but-none-in-Redhill argument seems to emphasise the side of a Borough where progress was not made in the 19th century and highlight it against all those other things that were achieved. Perhaps many achievements were no more than effects of a growing Borough in which progress carried most before it, being forced to roll over certain immovable attitudes and leave them behind.

The End of an Era

This history has reached the end of the nineteenth century, having been written at the end of the twentieth. The rest of the story, that of the events of the twentieth century will be written at the beginning of the twenty-first.

The ends of historical eras are not heralded by the calendar but by those events which have the greatest impact on people's lives. 1901 was the year of the death of Queen Victoria, our longest ever reigning monarch, and the start of the Edwardian Age, a period of which is said that attitudes and behavioural changes stamped a new character upon the country.

Whether this is true or not depends upon the rate of those changes, for change is one thing that older people tend to be wary of and therefore resist, it being the young who embrace new freedoms with enthusiasm and carry them through their own generation and into the next.

We have just been discussing the Town Clerk, a man who had known the area at a time when Redhill did not exist; who had witnessed the railways being built, had taken part in the drive for incorporation and had been the most closely involved of any man in local affairs for close to forty years. If there was anything about Redhill that he did not know then it was probably not worth knowing. He was now no doubt looking forward to a new century and wondering what differences it would bring to the lives of himself and those around him, as we who stand at the threshold of another new century do likewise. There is also a new millennium but few of us would venture to look beyond the first tenth of that.

As far as the Twentieth Century has been concerned we now know just what change was in store. The Great War altered perspectives forever, and in a way that people would never forget. If those who lived through that war had known there was an even greater war to come only twenty years hence they would have realised that the first half of their new century was going to shake up the old ways and create for itself a second half vastly different from the first.

In-between times many other subjects dominated the local news and occupied people's minds, and many non-headline sagas unfolded over the years. The stories of St Anne's, the Gas and Water companies, the Surrey Mirror, the Telephone service, public houses, the bus service; the controversy surrounding the centralisation of Borough Council offices, the various schemes for a lasting war memorial (also controversial), the growth of the cinemas, the Borough's own electricity supply, the rebuilding of Redhill, the Tristan Da Cuhnans, the changes in Borough boundaries to include Horley and Gatton, and later Kingswood, Tadworth and Banstead - all these and much more has been the Twentieth Century in this town of Redhill, and there is still a great deal more of the story still to be told.

Brief Chronology

1066	Battle of Hastings
1085/6	Domesday Survey and Book
1150	Approximate date of founding of Reigate Town
1300	The name 'Redehelde', for Redhill Common Hill, in use
1390	First mention of Holegehe (Hooley) sub-manor
1659	Civil War skirmish on Redhill Common
1675	Reigate Grammar School founded on its present site
1699	First turnpike road in Surrey, Reigate to Crawley
1700	Earliest record of Blackborough Mill
1728	Reigate Old Town Hall erected
1736	Date on beam of Blackborough Mill
1755	Present road up Reigate Hill built
1794	Workhouse built on Earlswood Common
1801	First census
1805	Surrey Iron Railway established
1806	Croydon, Merstham and Godstone railway opened
1808	London-Reigate road via Gatton built
1809	Forerunner of Borough Fire Brigade formed with the gift of two fire engines from Lords Hardwicke and Somers
1816	Gatton to Povey Cross road built
1817	Land granted for the Somers Arms to be built on corner of Mill Street and Brighton Road.
1823	Tunnel made under Castle Grounds, Reigate
1824	Wray Common Mill built
1830	Lord Monson acquired Gatton
1837	London-Brighton railway route sanctioned
1838	Reigate Gas Company formed
1839	Surrey Iron Railway taken out of use
1841	Service on London-Brighton railway began
1841	Death of Lord Monson
1841	Loss of coaching business closed Somers Arms

1842	Railway service to Tonbridge began
1843	St John's Church built
1843	Post office established at Whitepost Hill
1844	Railway service London-Dover began
1845	Eliza Cook writing poem about The Old Mill (in Mill Street?)
1846	Sale of leasehold plots of land by the Countess of Warwick - Warwick Town begins
1849	Royal Philanthropic Farm School opened
1849	Reading branch line built
1854	Ebenezer Hooper came to Redhill
1856	Post office moved to Station Road
1858	Railway Station named 'Red Hill Junction'
1859	Reigate Water Works Company formed
1859	First meeting in the movement for Incorporation
1860	Redhill Market House (Hall) built
1861	Census reveals that population of Redhill and Reigate had doubled in 10 years to 10,000
1861	Newspaper excise duty and taxes abolished
1861	St Joseph's Church opened
1861	Chapel of Ease of St. Matthew's opened
1861	Royal Earlswood Asylum opened by Prince of Wales
1861	Reigate Public Hall built
1862	Sixteen acres on top of Red Hill Common purchased by the War office for a military prison
1862	Congregational Church opened
1863	Borough of Reigate created by grant of Charter of Incorporation
1863	First elections of Council members
1864	Borough police force formed
1865	Redhill Gas Company formed
1865	Redhill fire brigade formed
1866	St Matthew's Church consecrated
1866	Reigate and Redhill Hospital opened

1867	Mains water laid to Redhill	1884	Prince of Wales laid foundation stone of St Anne's chapel
1867	Sixteen acres on top of Redhill Common bought from War office	1884	St Anne's officially opened by Sir R.N.Fowler, Lord Mayor of London.
1867	Death of Thomas Martin, last bailiff of Reigate	1884	Redhill became forwarding centre for mail for the area bounded by London, Reading and Dover. Large Sorting office built at the station.
1867	Sewerage and drainage of Redhill completed		
1867	Mains water pipes laid to Redhill by the Caterham Spring Water Company	1887	Queen Victoria's Golden Jubilee
1869	Reigate Borough's own Justice of the Peace formed	1888	Sir Jeremiah Colman bought Gatton estate from Monson family
1870	Market House Company went into liquidation	1889	St John's Church rebuilt
1871	Market Hall Company formed.	1891	Post office opened in Market Hall extension. Jennings' sub-post office closed.
1876	Drinking fountain outside Market Hall		
1881	End of the toll roads	1892	West Wing of Market Hall built
1882	Court case stops digging on Redhill Common and forms body of Conservators	1894	Redhill Football Club formed
		1895	Population of Redhill about 13,500
1883	Mill Street pleasure gardens laid out	1896	Inaugural car run through Borough
1884	First sod turned by Mayor Robert Field on site for building of St Anne's	1897	Queen Victoria's Diamond Jubilee
		1897	Sports Ground opened

Redhill F.C. 1899

Glossary

Brief and very general descriptions of some terms used in this history

Manor

The administrative area of Reigate before the modern Borough of Reigate came into being in 1863. The Manor was in two parts; a central 400-acre area known as Reigate Old Borough, and a second 6000-acre around it called the Foreign. Knowledge of the original formation of the Manor is obscured by the mists of time.

Reigate Old Borough

The chief borough of Reigate Manor, containing Reigate town.

Reigate Old Town

Similar to the above.

The Foreign

The area of the Manor other than the central, or main, Borough. The Foreign contained the additional boroughs of Colley, Hooley, Santon, Woodhatch and Linkfield. In addition there were sub-manors carved out of Reigate Manor, such as Frenches, Redstone and the Priory.

Petty Boroughs

Boroughs other than Reigate Old Borough.

Lord of the Manor

The person who held title to the lands of the Manor. Over the centuries title passed from the first Norman Lord of the Manor, William de Warenne, through various hands to the Somers family who retained extensive ownership of property in Reigate after the formation of the Borough of Reigate. The last Lord of the Manor was Mr Somers Somerset, who sold his property in Reigate Town in 1921 and presented the remainder of his manorial interests to the Corporation in 1922. The Corporation is now effectively Lord of the Manor for any lingering administrative matters.

Parish

The area administered by the church, of which in early manorial days St Mary's was the only one. The Parish had boundaries similar to the Manor.

Vestry

A body administering the ecclesiastical affairs of the Parish. In addition it administered some public affairs, such as the Poor Rate. There were two vestries, one for Reigate Old Borough and one for Reigate Foreign.

The foregoing may generally be of Norman origin, i.e. post Conquest. Probably of Saxon origin is: -

Tithing

An administrative district of a manor. Originally an ancient term referring to an area or group originally containing ten men or families who had responsibilities for each other in law.

The uses of 'Red Hill' and 'Redhill'.

'Red Hill' was the early name for the area generally containing the present Redhill Common. It was also the way the name of the new town was at first written. In the text the current form of 'Redhill' is mainly used for the town and is often also used for the common, just as it is today, but when the form 'Red Hill' is more appropriate then it is used instead.

References and Bibliography

This history is not annotated with chapter-by-chapter references as it might have been. Technically this would have been a good way to list sources and make pertinent remarks of my own but I soon found that the note points tended to interfere with the text flow and the chapter-end lists were unwieldy. I also felt that as the majority of readers picking up this book would probably be doing so for interest alone I should make it as easy to read as possible. I therefore made the decision not to include footnotes, and the space saved by their removal was speedily used to include more subject material.

So where did all the information come from? As stated in the introduction to this history the sources are various; they include archives, books, newspapers, personal reminiscences and the like, all of which give a flavour of times past; the vast majority supplying direct information. It is exciting indeed to discover new information; very satisfying to discover a second, different source to verify the first; intriguing and challenging to find varying accounts of the same events. Below is a reference list, bibliography and miscellaneous list of information sources that have supplied me with these experiences.

Additional to listed items are those sources which may not be so repeatable or accessible in the future. These include talks I have had with people with specialised knowledge of aspects of Redhill's past; access I have enjoyed to records and collections not generally available to the public; meetings, events, symposia and exhibitions on local history which may not be repeated; and sight (and often extended loan) of material in private hands. No one should be deterred from research, however, just because not all relevant material is immediately to hand. I found much that I was at first totally unaware of, and I am certain there is a great deal more to be found - which is good because I have not yet finished looking.

AJM

References

BT Archives; London
BT Museum; London
County Records Office   - Churchwardens' Accounts
     - Library, various titles
     - Police, annual reports
     - Reigate Borough Council, minutes of full council meetings
     - Reigate Borough Council, Watch Committee minutes
     - Vestry meeting minutes
     - Royal Philanthropic Society, reports 1848-1975
     (Consult the index of their holdings, there's much more)
Holmesdale Natural History Club, Reigate, Local History section
National Newspaper Library, Colindale
Redhill Library   - Family History Section, Census returns
     - Local History Section, various books and records
Reigate Priory Museum, exhibitions
Royal Earlswood Hospital, archives
Shoreditch High Street Library, London Telephone Books (inc. Redhill subscribers) 1893 -99
Surrey Fire Preservation Trust Museum
Surrey Mirror Archives

Bibliography

The Archaeology of Surrey to 1500, Editors J. & D.G.Bird, 1987
A Guide to the Industrial History of Reigate and Banstead, Derek Stidder, 1996
A Hand-book to Reigate, R.F.D.Palgrave, 1860 (reprinted 1973)
A History of Reigate Priory, Ernest Scears. C1950

Bibliography

A History of the Royal Philanthropic Society 1788-1988, Revised 1988, The RPS
A Short History of Reigate Borough Fire Brigade, F.Legg, 1935?
Blake, Palmer, Linnell & Co. The Life of John Linnell, David Linnell, 1994
Cherchefelle and the Origins of Reigate, R.Poulton, 1980
The Country Around Reigate and Dorking, HMSO, 1933
Discovering Reigate Priory, The Place and the People, Audrey Ward, 1999
East Surrey Then and Now, Mark Davison 1992
Geological, Historical and Topographical Description of the Borough of Reigate, R.Phillips, 1885
Handbook to the Environs of London, James Thorne, 1876
Industrious Surrey, Chris Shepheard and the Surrey Industrial History Group, 1994
Introduction to the Postal History of Reigate, Redhill and District, L.Britnor & A.Latham, 1973
Laws and Bye-Laws of the Borough of Reigate, various dates
Memories of Yesterday, Alan Ingram and Malcolm Pendrill, 1984
Our Homestead (about Wiggie), Arthur Trower,
Papers of the Surrey Local History Council, various volumes, numerous years
People of Reigate and St Mary's from 1500-1930, Audrey Taylor, 1988
Redhill as a Railway Centre, E.F.Carter, 1955
Redhill At War, The Lighter Side, Geoffrey Tait and Paul Smith, 1984
Redhill, the Rise of a Railway Town in the Nineteenth Century, paper by Derek Wickham, 1982
Reflections of Yesterday, Alan Ingram and Malcolm Pendrill, 1982
Reigate and Redhill Past and Present, Keith Harding, 1998
Reigate and Redhill, Mary Goss, 1995
Reigate, Home and Foreign, Past and Present, Harcourt Burrage, 1901
Reigate, Its Story Through the Ages, Wilfrid Hooper, 1945
Retracing The First Public Railway (Living History Guide No.4) Derek Bayliss, 1981
Social Scenes of Yesterday, Alan Ingram, 1992
Surrey At Work In Old Photographs, Chris Shepheard, 1992
Surrey Within Living Memory, Surrey Federation of Women's Institutes, 1992
The Barons' Caves, a Guide, Peter Burgess, 1994
The Brighton Run, Lord Montagu of Beaulieu, Shire Album 251
The Business Guide to Redhill, Reigate and Horley, 1891
The Doctor's Tale, 1662-1975, Reigate and Redhill, Lawrence Dulake, 1976
The History of Frenches Cricket Club, John Barton
The History of Merstham, H.M.Morris, 1971
The History of the Reigate Borough Police force, 1864-1947, Richard Ford, 1973
The Holmesdale Pictorial Guide to Redhill and Reigate, 1924
The Redhill Story, Nigel Dunne, 1994
Towns of Character, W.A.Hutchinson, 1985
Up The Reds, The History of Redhill Football Club, 1884-94, Brian Thomas, 1994
Victoria History of Surrey
Victorian Almshouse Reigate and Redhill 1897-1997, John Wilkins

Additionally there are many more books dealing with Reigate and Merstham which contain information relevant to Redhill. I am as certain that this list does not contain everything I have read, as I am equally sure it does not contain everything I should have read.

Miscellaneous

Borough of Reigate official guides, various dates; church magazines; church histories; handbooks or guides to the local area (and there have been quite a few over the years); histories of local hospitals, various dates; maps; magazine articles; programmes to local events, various dates; Shire book series, various titles; street directories (Holmesdale, Kelly's, Allingham's) various dates; timetables.

Index

To my wife Muriel
Thanks for everything